"I always look forward to hearing what William Kenower has to say about writing. In his latest book, Kenower explores what it means to be a successful creative as he examines the equality of personal talent. As usual, I felt energized and validated by his intellectual discussion of prose and life. Kenower reminds us to enjoy the whole writing journey, not just the high points. *Everyone Has What It Takes* will give your creative side a much-needed boost, which is good, because, as Kenower says, ' . . . the page is waiting for you.'"

—Windy Lynn Harris, author of
Writing & Selling Short Stories & Personal Essays

"Like Elizabeth Gilbert in *Big Magic,* Bill Kenower teaches us that sometimes the simplest ideas are the most profound. *Follow your curiosity. Lead your life. Write your books.* In honest, accessible prose, Kenower takes us past craft and into the psyche, where all writing starts, and gives us the core lessons that every writer needs to hear, and probably every day."

—Erica Bauermeister, bestselling author of
The School of Essential Ingredients and *The Scent Keeper*

"William Kenower's encouraging new book, full of personal tales and relatable wisdom, urges you to throw out everything you think you know about becoming a successful writer. Instead, he exhorts, be curious, trust your words, say yes to opportunities and, most important, keep writing what matters to you. A must-read for writers at all stages of the process."

—Jordan Rosenfeld, author of *How to Write a Page-Turner*

"William Kenower offers engaging personal stories from his personal experience about how, as writers, we often put ourselves on what I'd call 'a failure to thrive' track. Then he expertly shows us how to reverse that toward pleasure and finding our own writing path."

—Sheila Bender, author of *Writing Personal Essays*

"In *Everyone Has What It Takes*, Bill Kenower reminds us that with the right mind-set and attitude, we can create our own success with our writing. Using poignant stories from his life, Kenower shines light on the negative things we tell ourselves related to our creative life and illustrates a more positive approach for us to take. Inspiring and encouraging, this book should be part of every writer's library."

—Kerrie Flanagan, writing consultant and author of *The Writer's Digest Guide to Magazine Article Writing* and The Magazine Writing Blueprint

"William Kenower is the writing coach you've always wanted. In *Everyone Has What It Takes*, Kenower gives you the support you need to live your writing life without fear or worry. Through stories and examples, he shows you that you really do have what it takes to become a successful writer. I loved this book—it showed me a positive approach to writing that is less about competition and more about creativity and understanding. This book is about life, and the best way to live it—fully aware of who you are and who you want to be." —Kate Ristau, author of *Shadow Girl* and *Clockbreakers*

Everyone Has What It Takes

Everyone Has
What It Takes

A Writer's Guide to the End of Self–Doubt

William Kenower

**WRITER'S
DIGEST
BOOKS**

WRITER'S
DIGEST
BOOKS

An imprint of Penguin Random House LLC
penguinrandomhouse.com

ISBN 9780593330784
eBook ISBN 9780593330791

Printed in the United States of America
1st Printing

Book design by Ashley Tucker

For anyone who thinks they can't

The privilege of a lifetime is being who you are.

—JOSEPH CAMPBELL

Contents

Foreword

In my twenties, my boss turned to me unexpectedly during a live meeting when *she* was next up to speak, and asked, "Susie, do you want to present the business development overview this morning?"

I was startled. I shook my head no. *Um—no way! I've had no time to overprepare, worry, and overthink, thank you very much!*

She smiled and went ahead and presented it herself as usual.

All day I wrestled with that no.

What was it that made me turn down the chance to step up?

Regrettably, I knew the answer. I didn't want to screw around, stumble, or say something wrong. I didn't even want to *blush*. I wasn't willing to experience any discomfort or make a mistake.

She didn't ask again—not the next meeting, or the next. It

ate me up a little bit as the weeks passed. How could I go bigger in my life without saying yes to more?

I promised myself that if she asked me again, I'd say yes.

Each meeting I'd go in, a bit nervous—wanting (but also *not* wanting!) her to ask me again. I was prepared each week.

One week, she did ask again. I said yes.

I presented the report almost every week after that.

Why the shift?

Because I was willing to do just one thing. *Be uncomfortable*. Risk getting it wrong. Take a chance that I could screw it up.

And that, my friend, is all confidence is.

This book will help you bypass the no that you wrestle with a lot of the time (we've all been there).

Most people won't tell you this, but some opportunities don't pass by a second time.

Most important—your life doesn't. As the old saying goes, this isn't a dress rehearsal. The time to write is now.

And your contribution as a writer is so much bigger than to just yourself. As you learn to believe in yourself, you teach others to believe in themselves, too. Success is generous. Whenever you step up to be, do, have, and create more—you silently give everyone in your life permission to do so as well. Read this book not just for you but for the thousands of other self-doubters you'll encounter in your life.

We all have what it takes. But we all don't use what we have. This book will help you regret-proof your life.

I wish every writer could encounter Bill Kenower's wisdom,

compassion, and savvy. This might be the best gift you ever give yourself, and the world.

With so much love from one writer to another,
Susie Moore

CHAPTER ONE

A New Story

I discovered the pleasure of writing when I was nine, which I have since learned is about the average age of discovery for most writers. This was the same time I was learning how to do a lot of different things—ride a bike, play football, add fractions, draw soldiers and tanks—but of all these things, only writing stood out to me as something I might want to keep doing when I grew up. For one, I seemed to be pretty good at it. How did I know this? The same way I knew I was good at anything back then: An adult told me so. Also, even though writing was something I learned how to do in school, I was happy to do it when I was out of school, which meant it didn't feel like work.

As a teenager I became quite serious about wanting to be a professional writer. Adults, and sometimes even my friends, still complimented my writing, but a quiet question had begun to worm its way into my mind. Did they mean I was *actually* good at this, or simply good for a teenager? If they found my stories in a magazine, would they feel the same about them? That, it seemed to me, was how you *knew* you were good, that you had what it took to be a "real" writer.

By the time I was twenty, a college composition professor had told me he looked forward to reading the reviews of my work in the *New York Times*. I'd also written a short story I was particularly pleased with. It was based on meeting and losing a girl I loved. It was the first time I'd written about something from my own life. Also, the ending surprised me. It was like the story had shown me why I was writing it. That was the first time that had ever happened. When I showed it to my mom—as I did all my stories then—she took it into her bedroom to read in private. When she finished, she chirped, "Oh! That's *good!*" And when my friend Gorham read it, he said, "That's like a story I'd read in a magazine." A writing teacher applauded when I finished reading it in class.

And so, did I *know* then I was good enough, that I had what it took? Had all that praise and positivity answered that question once and for all? Not *quite*. I couldn't sell the story, or the next one I wrote. I eventually published some poems, but just three. When I wrote and performed a play and it got laughs and applause, it was still only in little dusty theaters in Providence. And when I was a quarterfinalist for the Nicholl Fellowships in screenwriting, I didn't actually *win*.

Then I started writing novels. I was twenty-five and the novel occupied a special category in my mind. If you published a novel, then you absolutely had what it took. No question. Unfortunately, my first novel didn't sell, and my second novel didn't sell, and then my third novel did sell, but only to a tiny, tiny, tiny, barely existent publisher. And then my fourth novel didn't sell, either. With every passing year and with every unpublished book, the questions grew louder and louder in my mind: What if I don't have what it takes? What if all this failure and disappointment is the consequence of some inherent deficiency in me? What if I am like a fish trying to climb a tree? No matter how much I *wanted* to reach the top, I was bound to Earth by my nature.

In the middle of all this, my youngest son, Jack, was diagnosed on the autism spectrum. Like most kids on the spectrum, he would retreat into an inner world where he was difficult to reach. I soon learned that the only way I could parent him was if I didn't see him as broken and try to fix him. I couldn't become transfixed by his odd behavior; I had to see beyond that veil to the whole person who always lay beneath it. Except it was impossible for me to see *him* as whole, this kid who hummed and thumped on his chest when he was nervous, if I saw myself as broken because I wasn't successful, or if I saw someone else as broken because they were unkind. The only way I could see Jack as unbroken was if no one was broken—period.

Learning to see people this way became a kind of practice. It wasn't easy. Sometimes the world seemed positively filled with broken people—all the cruelty and corruption and violence and failure and misery. I saw it. I saw it all. But because of this practice, because I wanted to be Jack's dad, because of love, I began to see those people differently, too. After all, I didn't *want* to live in a world with broken people. No one does. What if we already lived in the world we wanted, but we just hadn't learned how to see it?

Then one day, after several years of this practice, I sat down to write. The question of whether I had what it took still swirled in my mind. How could it not? I was a middle-aged man who had spent most of my adult life working as a waiter to support my family. But something had begun to change in me. In certain ways my practice with Jack reminded me of writing. I wasn't really learning to *see* a world without broken people, I was practicing going to a place within myself where I *couldn't* see broken people because from that place, in that place, they simply didn't exist.

Meanwhile, every time I sat down to write, my first goal was to forget about the world I lived in and find that place within myself where stories emerged. I loved that place. I couldn't always find it, but when I did, the ideas of right and wrong and good and bad dissolved, replaced only by what belonged in my story and what did not. It was a place of inspiration and support, for when I was there ideas came *to* me, I didn't go get them. When the writing went well, I didn't so much make something as find it and describe it.

On this day, the writing went very well. I had by this time shifted away from fiction and begun writing regularly about the link between spirituality and creativity. When I finished the essay I was working on, I sat back and took a moment to enjoy that calm, alive stillness with which you are left when you've gone deep down into the writing rabbit hole. It's like coming home, this friendly, inviting place. Everyone's welcome there.

That's when I realized that where I went to write felt almost exactly like the place I went to see a world without broken people. This got my attention. For how often had I looked in the mirror after the umpteenth rejection and asked, "What's wrong with me?" No answer ever came. What if the answer never came because there was none? What if I couldn't figure out if *I* had what it took, if I was one of the lucky, gifted

What if everyone has what it takes?

ones, because there were no lucky, gifted ones? What if *everyone* has what it takes?

So much of writing and creativity is about asking yourself compelling questions. *What if I could fly? Why does my hero love that girl? Why did I feel estranged from my father?* These are the kinds of questions from which stories are born, the kinds of questions we ask and answer and ask and answer as we wind our way sentence by sentence or stanza by stanza through our day's work. The better and more interesting the question— and the more clearly the question is framed—the better the answer, the better the work.

However, the question "Do I have what it takes?" is the worst kind of question. We only ask it because we believe there might be some answer other than "Yes!" And yet the idea that the answer could be "No" is intolerable. It's like asking if our nightmares are real or if we deserve to be loved. Simply asking the question opens you to the possibility that you might somehow lack what you need to succeed at what you most want to do, to live the life you most want to live.

All those years I found no success as a novelist, I was plagued by that unanswerable question. The success I have found since has come in large part because I learned I never needed to ask it, that the question itself had been like static obscuring my access to the stories I most want to tell. I have found that I love teaching and talking to writers about writing. The more I do so, the more I learn that this question of those who have what it takes and those who do not permeates the writing community like an unspoken rule, a doctrine we have adopted out of an unconscious allegiance to some master whose only desire is to see the world of people divided.

Yet the temptation to divide the world into creative haves and have-nots is great, and in some ways, pragmatic. After all, the stories of failure and disappointment in writing and in the arts and just in life, period, are legion. You need only open your eyes for a moment and look around to see it. If you spend any time around writers, you will meet those people who start but never finish a story, or who finish one and can't find an agent, or whose books are published but barely sell. Or you might find yourself talking to professional writers and discover many of them mired in a quiet despair, feeling that whatever success they've managed to scratch out is never enough. They'll tell you it's a brutal business, that only the lucky or the geniuses or the total sellouts make any money at it.

Then, of course, there are your own experiences. You're not just a writer, you're also a reader. How often have you read an article or short story, or started a book, and thought, *This guy sucks*? How often have you found that what you're reading or watching or listening to is boring or forced or predictable and thought that whoever made it should find something else to do? If you are like me, you may find that there is no more irritating an experience than consuming a story or song or movie you dislike. Why, you might ask, can't more writers write like your favorite authors? Why does this other stuff exist? Clearly there's good stuff and bad stuff. I can see it and hear it with my own ears and eyes. I know it because I love this stuff and absolutely *hate* that other stuff. Clearly the world of the arts, of creations, *is* divided into those who have the ability to make good stuff, and those who most definitely do *not*.

Finally, there is that private, miserable experience of wondering if you are one of those who do not have what it takes. You can't finish a story, or you can't start a story, or you get to the middle and you can't remember why you started it. It's the worst feeling. You feel dead inside. You go looking for ideas and find nothing. There's nothing in you anymore. Where did the ideas go? You don't know, you just know how awful you feel and you would do anything to feel differently. If it gets really bad, you begin to understand stories of people selling their souls for a little success. Anything to end that lifeless misery. Anything to feel alive and interested and creative again. Anything to feel valuable again, lovable again. Why did you ever start trying to make something? Maybe you shouldn't have. Maybe you just don't have what it takes.

I know firsthand how dark it can get if we let it. When there's darkness within, you'll see nothing but shadow outside of you. As with my son, I've come to understand that seeing a world where everyone has what it takes is a constant practice, a practice that begins with me. I cannot see what I don't believe exists. I cannot perceive in others what I don't believe exists in myself; moreover, I also cannot believe I have something no one else has. I've lived both ends of this lie. One moment I'm everything, the next I'm nothing; one moment I'm the king, the next I'm a peasant.

I spend a lot of time talking to writers of all experience levels. On some days, it feels like they're the only people I ever talk to. I'm even married to a writer. As a rule, we are a tender, kind bunch. There are a few cranks who let their disappointment seep out, but mostly writers are supportive and helpful to one another. I see it every time I go to a conference or teach a workshop or conduct an interview. All of which has only reinforced how difficult this concept of equality truly is. For even within this warm community, this accepting community, this inclusive community, there is this constant division, between the Great Writers and the schlubs, the geniuses and the hacks, the bestsellers and the mid-listers. Every time we divide ourselves in this way, we make accessing our own unique genius that much harder.

If I had to give a writer only one piece of advice, it wouldn't be to hone their craft or buy a writing book or go to a writers' conference. The best piece of advice I could give a writer now, having been on this journey for many years, would be to walk down any street and try to see themselves as no better and no *worse* than anyone, not the panhandler or the guy in the BMW. I would also advise the writer to practice this while walking through a bookstore, past the stories they love and all the stories they do not. Know that someone loves the story you hate, and someone hates the story you love, and that everyone is right.

It's not so easy to see the world this way. Many authors write secretly to raise themselves to a height from which they can be seen by many, to be lauded and revered as they themselves have lauded and revered *their* favorite authors. But in truth, writing is a deep dive into our inherent, inescapable equality, into what connects us and makes everyone human.

I hope this book will help you in this practice. Everything you really need to know is contained in its title, which is a little like calling a mystery *The Butler Did It*. Except everyone having what it takes is a mystery I keep solving and solving and solving. You can't solve it once. I solve it every time I meet another person, whether they're a writer or a banker or a toddler. Which is why this book is as much about living as it is about writing. Writing has helped me see people as they are, and seeing people as they are has helped me write. Writing has taught me how to live, and living has taught me how to write.

I don't know anything about you. I don't know how old you are or what you like to read and write or where you went to school or who you love or who you've lost. But I do know that only you can lead your life, just as only you can write your books. If you don't have what it takes to lead the life you want to lead, to write the book you want to write, then what's the point of even getting up in the morning? I can't think of one. So, think of this book as a kind of bedtime story. It's the story of how you've always had what it takes, how you've always been good enough and smart enough and talented enough, how there is no opposite of you, and if you like the story, if you believe the story, you can wake up ready to write your book and lead your life.

CHAPTER TWO

Choose What Fits

When I was eight, my teacher took our class out to the playground, lined us up, and told us to race to the brick wall at the other end of the yard. The brick wall was to be our finish line, a metaphor perhaps lost on the teacher at the moment. Nonetheless, we all put our toes on the starting line, and the teacher counted down and shouted, "Go!"

Go I did. It felt so good to run as fast as I could possibly run: to summon all my strength and ask the separate parts of my body, my legs and arms and lungs and feet, to work together for one purpose. And it felt good to be racing the others—for this goal, this finish line, this competition, gave my running a focus it was not otherwise easy to find. When I touched the wall, I looked across and saw that I had finished first.

Yet at that moment I understood, in my little eight-year-old mind, that the only reason I'd won was because I had *wanted* to run more than the others. I could feel in their bodies and faces that confusion and disinterest I had felt in myself when I had been asked to do something I wasn't all that interested in doing but that I nonetheless believed I must do very well. I didn't believe that my body was *biologically* faster than everyone else's body. I believed I better understood how to bring all my attention to my body and to running without any distraction.

This, I think, was the absolutely perfect relationship to tests of any kind, a relationship I could not maintain throughout much of my childhood when it seemed I was given tests as regularly as baths. Most of what I was tested on were things in which I was not personally interested. No matter. I would become good at being good at things, which is a great skill to have in school where you are asked to perform in many unrelated disciplines. I could climb the ropes, sink the basket, catch the pass, solve the equation, write the essay, dissect the frog. This is not the best skill, however, for writers, or for anyone who wants to be happy more than they're unhappy. School could not teach me this lesson. To learn it, I had to understand that I had taught myself to endure unhappiness, and that this was one more thing I could be good at.

Shortly after I left the restaurant where I had been working as a waiter for nearly twenty years, I bought a pair of black dress shoes. I loved those shoes. They were shiny and slick and their hard wooden soles made a satisfying clacking sound when I strutted around the house in them. I felt successful whenever I put them on. The only problem was they didn't seem to fit *exactly*. There was a slight pinch in the heel and toes. No matter. I decided they just needed to be broken in, that with enough walking they'd adapt themselves to me. When, after a few months of walking, they appeared set in their ways, I decided a slight pinch here and there was a small price to pay for such fabulous shoes. Plus, now that I wasn't a waiter, my life did not involve a lot of walking.

At that time, I was also still writing novels. I loved *writing* as much as ever, but more and more writing those stories felt like swimming against a current. What felt effortless one day was hard the next—though *hard* is maybe not even the right word. When I was going against the current, writing actually felt *impossible*, like I didn't know how to do it, that I'd not so much forgotten how to write as just remembered that I *never* knew how to write. This made no sense to me. I had a vague memory of feeling as if I was being carried by the current of the story I was telling, of riding that current and following it where it wanted to go. That had happened, hadn't it? Maybe I just needed to work harder, battle against the current the way I used to run up hills to strengthen my legs when I was a sprinter. Maybe I just needed to get *better*; maybe I wasn't battling against an enigmatic current but rather struggling with some technical weakness that, once corrected, would send me on my way.

So, I wrote on, struggling and battling. I'd have a good day and think, *That's it! I've solved it.* Then I'd have another bad day and I'd feel like a fraud, like the good days were a mirage I'd imagined in my creative desert. No matter. I wrote on. I wrote every day, good or bad, reasoning, *Well, this is how it goes. This is what life is like if you're a writer.*

That summer I was hired by a crazily successful video game company to write story lines for their games and to help them explore the possibility of publishing books. They were paying me what seemed like a lot of money for my consultation, which I quite liked, though I didn't particularly love coming up with the stories. Still, it was fun to be working with these very successful people, having meetings in offices, wearing nice clothes, and just being paid to write and think rather than serve steaks.

The company really wanted to publish book versions of their games, so they decided to send me and two other guys to New York to meet with a handful of literary agents to explore the possibility. New York! I had just the shoes for New York. They flew me out and put me up at an expensive hotel right next to Grand Central Terminal. I had an expense account for meals.

All the meetings were scheduled for the same day. That morning I put on my new shoes, met my comrades for breakfast, and headed out. We cabbed all over Manhattan, from agency to agency. By the second meeting I found walking up a flight of stairs a little uncomfortable, but soon I was sitting in a conference room, and I was fine. By the fourth meeting I was starting to anticipate with some dread the short walk from the cab to the office building. By the fifth and last meeting I was looking forward to returning to my hotel room, where a pair of sneakers waited for me. But when we stepped out onto the street, Charlie, our de facto leader, said, "Hey, it's a nice day. What if we skip the cab and just walk?"

"No problem!" I said, because I didn't want to seem fussy. And so, I began to walk.

It was only a mile or so. I'd be fine. My work for the day was done, and I'd let myself enjoy the afternoon, the brisk hustle of the city, the one-of-a-kind skyline, the whole New Yorkness of it, thereby distracting myself from the shoes, which were hurting me even when I simply stood in them. It took me only one block to understand that no city in the world could distract me from what those shoes inflicted with every single step. I found myself focusing on the momentary relief one foot experienced as my stride lifted it off the ground on its way forward. That walk to the hotel became an endurance test. My entire existence was reduced to the pain I was experiencing and the freedom to which every searing step brought me closer. There was a moment, while still a half mile from the hotel, when I considered taking them off and finishing the walk in my stocking feet. It was tempting, but I couldn't be that guy, the guy in a blazer carrying his shoes through New York, so I walked on, fantasizing with every stride of the hotel room and my coming shoelessness.

I made it, dear reader. I made it. My feet survived, and the moment I pulled off those loafers it was like being freed from two bear traps. I exhaled and lay back on my bed, reacquainting myself to life without pain. This, I was reminded, is how I was meant to live. I had never appreciated my feet in their natural state as much as I did then. I was to meet my brother, who lived in Brooklyn, for dinner. When he showed up, I actually deliberated briefly about what to wear, not liking how

I'd look wearing slacks and sneakers—but the memory of the walk back to the hotel was fresh enough that I decided fashion be damned.

It was the right choice. Those first few steps out the door of the hotel room and down the hall toward the elevator were a revelation. Every time one of my sneakered feet hit the floor, a wave of gratitude washed through me. I'd forgotten how nice walking could be. But then we reached the elevator and were talking about where to go for dinner, and how we'd meet up with some old friends, and that he wanted to hear some stories from my adventures in the city. By the time we'd ridden the elevator to the lobby and were headed out into the evening, walking was just walking again, how I got from one place to the other, not something to dread or appreciate.

The video game company never did publish any books, and I quit working with them by the fall and started an online magazine for writers called *Author*. It would, however, be another couple of years until I quit writing novels. That final stretch was like the last quarter mile in New York before I reached the hotel. Except that until the very *moment* I said, "That's enough—I'm done with fiction," I continued to believe that the freedom and relief of which I so often dreamed, the end of my suffering, would arrive with the publication of my first novel. It was as if I thought that the shoes weren't the problem, *I* was the problem, that like Cinderella's sisters I could fit myself into the preconceived trappings of the life I wanted.

This was the first step, so to speak, in understanding that I had what it took. I sometimes envy my artist and writer friends who tell me they had become painters or actors or poets because there was nothing else they were any good at. It simplifies things. Because while I know these friends suffered off and on with feelings of inferiority stemming from the memory, particularly as children, of failing the math test or being picked last in gym or being bad at whatever day job they managed to find, in actuality, the apparent narrowness of their skill is not a deficiency but rather an acute reflection of something that is true for all of us.

As someone who acquired a lot of skill at a lot of things, I have come to the firm conclusion that ability alone has little to do with what we call success. Skill, or talent, is a manifestation of focus, not something inherent in anyone like eye color or height. What's more, people can focus on anything, even things they hate. I've found myself watching a movie for an hour before I realized I wasn't actually enjoying it. No one told me to watch it, but because I was bored or because I didn't feel like looking for something else, I just sat there focusing on this story I was gradually repelled by. This is how I could become pretty good at things I was not interested in.

Ability alone has little to do with what we call success.

But to find real, authentic, satisfying success with anything, you must be able to do this thing again and again for a very long time. Books can take years to write, and a writing career is comprised of many books, essays, or stories. What you choose to focus on, the stories you choose to tell, must be a good fit. Unlike a pair of shoes, which can fit millions of people with the same size feet, the stories you should tell will fit only you. Period. Like it or not, we are all as unique as we are equal.

It is impossible to overstate how important this is, and also how strangely illusive to believe. When we say we *have* what it takes, that thing we *have* does not exist the way something does in the physical world. In the physical world, if you have something, you can hold it in your hand or sit on it or share it with someone else. If you have something, you can lose it or someone can take it from you. Also, there might not be a lot of it. You might have one of only four Honus Wagner trading cards. If someone won an award for which you were also nominated, that someone now has something you might have wanted. Loss and gain, more and less, are the boundaries and measurements of the world of things, what we all share and steal and point to and praise and argue about and covet and disregard.

The key to your success, however, is your curiosity—the unique, inherent, ceaseless mechanism of your interest. It is like a magnet for your focus, what allows you to turn your attention to something without resistance. You have it, but no one else can see it or touch it. You have it, but you can't lose it; you can only ignore it. You have it, but you can't change it or control it or command it; you can only follow it. This is why it is so hard to believe sometimes that everyone has what it takes. If everyone had a puppy, everyone could show theirs to everyone else. But our curiosity exists where only we can experience it. I cannot see yours and you cannot see mine. All we see are the products of that curiosity.

One of the biggest differences between professional writers and beginning writers is that the professional writer has learned, whether intuitively or, like me, through decades of trial and error, to follow that curiosity wherever *it* wants to go, not where *they* think it should go. As the editor of *Author* and the host of a podcast (*Author2Author*), I've interviewed hundreds of writers of all types—science fiction writers, suspense writers, romance writers, memoirists, screenwriters. Their books are all very different, not just from genre to genre but within the genres themselves. What is not different, however, is the "formula" they followed for their success. While some outlined and some dove straight in and some got a master's of fine arts degree and some toiled in their mother's basement, *all* of them wrote the kind of book they most wanted to write, that was interesting to them and them alone for reasons they could not wholly explain. So often I have heard this experience of an idea lighting up for someone described in more or less the same way that I might find it boring if it were not the animating spark for life itself.

A couple things about curiosity. First, while I can choose what I focus on, and can also choose whether I will give myself over to what I'm focusing on, I cannot choose what I'm curious about. I can only recognize this. What I'm curious about is chosen elsewhere. The difference is important and can be a little confusing. Part of the reason I *chose* to focus on novels was because that's what I used to read and because I knew I wanted to work in prose and not poetry or theater, and so being a novelist seemed to make intellectual sense. Yet I chose novels without having a story I was interested in telling. I just wanted to write sentences that told a story. I didn't ask myself, as I would much later, "If you could write anything at all, regardless of whether it was ever published, what would it be?"

I don't actually know what I would have answered back when I began my first novel. There was a brief time just before I started that first story when I tried to piece together what I wanted to write. I thought about what I liked about poetry and sketch comedy and short stories and screenwriting and tried to figure out how to pull together the best from each discipline—but I couldn't picture what that would be, and I was twenty-five, and I'd dropped out of college, and I was impatient, and "novelist" seemed like a good career, something I knew other people had done successfully, and so I thought, *I'll do that.*

This is the second thing about curiosity: Where it leads you might not fit nicely into a preconceived notion of a life. My older sister, Felicie, is a schoolteacher (a reading specialist, to be exact). Being a teacher had been her dream since she was a girl. This is where *her* curiosity led her. Felicie would have plenty of challenges in her life, as we all do, but picturing what her career would be like was not one of them. How I envied that. It was why I tried to be a novelist and why I even tried for about six months my freshman year at college to be a journalist. Journalist was a job a person who wrote could hold. But I couldn't pretend I wanted to be a journalist.

Now that I have been following my curiosity for a while, I

see plenty of other examples of people doing what I do, which is to write personal narrative, teach workshops, coach clients, and give inspiring talks. What fun. I also interview people. I do that, too. But when I started following my curiosity, *all* I saw was the path I was to follow. I didn't know where it was headed or what I would find there. I just knew it felt better to follow it than not.

Which is the third thing you have to know about curiosity: The only proof you really get that you're on the "right path" is that it feels good to follow it. There are no obstructions. In fact, it is true that sometimes ideas come to me that are so bright and strong I *must* pursue them, must get to my desk as quickly as possible and begin writing. This is how I felt when I saw for the first time the woman who is now my wife. I thought, *I have to meet her.* I felt like I had no choice.

But more often, an interesting idea is one whose appeal is simply that there's no obstruction, no resistance when I lay my attention on it. There are no cymbal crashes or fireworks. The path just looks clear. When I see these ideas, unlike with my wife, I feel like I *could* choose not to pursue them. They're not really calling to me, as we say. But when I lay my attention on them, there isn't anything calling me away, either. Focusing on these ideas is easy, effortless. Why, it doesn't really feel like work to explore them. Like those sneakers I finally wore in New York, following the idea just feels like walking.

This is how most of my success has been found. Yes, there have been some exciting moments where Big Ideas announced themselves, but mostly I found my success quietly, following the path of least resistance. The path of least resistance is not thrilling usually. If a path is really a good fit, it can be hard to recognize its value because it feels so natural. Doesn't success come from a lot of *hard work*? Not in my experience. It was *hard work* that taught me to follow my curiosity, which can only lead someplace I want to be.

So that's easy, right? Just follow your curiosity! Yes, and no. There are so many reasons we choose not to simply follow our curiosity, to not wholly trust what is unerringly trustworthy. I will get into them in detail throughout the rest of the book, though in general our unwillingness to trust has to do with time. As I said, I learned in school to get good at things I wasn't authentically interested in. I was not really a rebel as a boy. I enjoyed adults' approval, and I accepted that doing well in school—even in the things I would happily stop doing if someone older than me said I could—was somehow connected to my future success, which meant my future happiness.

I also quickly learned that it was easier to do something, *anything*, if I didn't fight it. That is, I would have rather spent an hour playing Wiffle Ball than practicing long division, but Wiffle Ball was not an option in math class, so division it was. However, if I gave myself over to the math, if I brought my focus to it without complaint, not only did I do better and learn quicker and receive that approval I seemed to require, but the math was also easier and, as experiences went, *not bad*.

Let me be clear: *Not bad* is a low bar for an experience. It is only a couple rungs up from "Get me out of here" or "Get these shoes off now!" *Not bad* is tolerable for a time, which is how I did well in school. I understood that school as a whole was temporary, that it would end about the same time adulthood began. What's more, the classes themselves were temporary. They were an hour long, five times a week, plus homework. Not too bad. And sometimes a little better than not too bad. I took physics when I was a junior in high school and rather enjoyed it. Sometimes I kind of looked forward to it.

Kind of liking is better than *not bad*, but only insofar as it takes longer for me to start hating what I kind of like, to start feeling the resistance more than the pleasure of focusing. Very soon, whatever I found not bad in school would become a kind of prison, through whose bars I could see a world of people I'm sure were having more fun than I.

This is how I spent twenty years writing novels I didn't really, truly want to write. Those novels were, however, a *very* close fit to the kinds of stories I wanted to tell. Excruciatingly close. They addressed in their own way what I would eventually address in the essays and books I write now: free will, creativity, God, death, unconditional love. But the form was not ideally suited to my voice. This is why it took so long for me to notice that I was uncomfortable, why I had to walk for twenty years in those shoes before I accepted that maybe this suffering wasn't normal, wasn't what life needed to feel like.

You are not *meant* to suffer. You almost certainly *will* suffer, as that is how you know when you are rejecting yourself, rejecting your own curiosity, your own life, in the same way the pinch in the shoe is how you know the shoe doesn't fit. The suffering, the discomfort, is information, guidance toward what fits you correctly. The suffering is not punishment; it's not proof of your worthlessness. It is trying to help you. If you listen to it, pay very close attention to it; the discomfort can be brief, sometimes as brief as a quick test-walk around the shoe store.

If you are like me, you have walked around the world in varying degrees of discomfort. You've worked a job you didn't really want to work, been in a relationship with someone you didn't really love, or tried to tell stories you didn't really want to tell. It's all right. Your imagination, your curiosity, your inherent interest aren't going anywhere. They're with you always. In fact, more than your hair or your beating heart, more even than the stories you write and the books you publish and see on bookshelves, your curiosity and your imagination *are* you. You are not that face in the mirror, not what casts a shadow on the wall. You are what asks and answers while writing, what dreams and remembers, what recognizes the light cast by something interesting to you and you alone. Look up from wherever you are, however dark and foreign the world feels, look up and follow it, and with that first step you take you will already be home.

CHAPTER THREE

Successful Experiences

I go to a lot of writers' conferences. I love them. So many earnest people gathered in one place because of a shared interest in writing and stories. Yet haunting every workshop and panel discussion is the formless specter of success—the very thing so many writers worry they do not have what it takes to achieve. Without success, the writing journey can appear meaningless. I've met more than a few students in workshops, usually men and women who came to writing in the middle of their life, whose primary objective is to learn if they're "any good." They don't want to bother pursuing something if it won't lead anywhere.

By "lead anywhere" these new writers almost always mean whether their stuff will get published. Publication can become a siren song, a kind of beacon on the hill pulling us forward even as it distracts us from the true nature of both success and what we have named failure. To be clear—I want to publish everything I write, to share what I find valuable, what I love, with other people. Sharing is not only fun, it's natural. Just as my children are not meant to live forever in my home, so too are my stories meant to travel beyond my desktop. Yet it wasn't until I started publishing regularly that I realized I had spent many years completely misunderstanding success itself.

I ATTENDED THE same writers' conference almost every year before I'd published my first book. It was exhilarating to be around so many other writers and to meet actual working authors, but I often felt as if an unwanted and nameless companion followed me from workshop to workshop. He was a downer, this companion. Never enjoying himself, he was always concerned what people thought about us. I'd have happily been rid of him, but I had a strange loyalty. As if years ago his mother had said, "Look after him, will you? He can't be left on his own." So, I dragged him around obediently, caring for something I hoped someday not to care for.

One year I was in the middle of working on a novel set in 1860s Missouri. It was the first story I'd ever attempted for which I had to do historical research, so I attended a panel on historical novels. One of the panelists was an author named Chris Kelley, which struck me because I had a close friend from childhood named Chris Kelley. This coincidence got my attention, and I found myself interested in whatever he had to say about research and stories and the writing life.

Once the panel was over, I decided to do something I

almost never did—I approached the author, Chris Kelley, and asked him some questions. I'm not a shy person, but that companion of mine usually reminded me that these authors were important people and that I shouldn't make a nuisance of myself. I ignored his advice that time, and asked my questions, which Chris Kelley happily answered. In fact, we talked about writing the way any two people interested in the same thing talk about anything. It was weirdly normal. At the end of our chat he shook my hand and said it was nice to meet me, and I said it was nice to meet him—once again, just the way normal people do. As I wandered out of the conference room, I said to my companion, "See? He's just a person. He talked to me just like a person talks to another person."

"That's only because he's named Chris Kelley," said my companion. "All Chris Kelleys talk to you like that."

My companion had his own distinctive logic.

A few months later I was talking to my wife about my woes, about how bad I felt sometimes about my life because of the books I wasn't selling, when I made this observation: "You know what, Jen? I think about writing differently than I think about everything else in my life, and not in a good way. It's screwy. I know it."

She agreed, but at the time I couldn't figure what that difference was. I could only feel it, some added pressure that was gumming up my thinking, making writing itself—the thing I actually loved doing—feel more mysterious and difficult than the rest of my life.

Years later, I was walking through a hotel parking lot on my way to that same writers' conference. I had just published my first book with a traditional publisher. I loved the book and would be teaching a few classes based on it. So much about this conference was familiar to me: the venue, the people running it, the agents and editors attending it. But as I approached the doors to the hotel, I realized something was very different. My companion wasn't with me. As I paused at the door, it was as if I could see him still, standing there, waiting perhaps for other writers—but not for me. It was only then that I understood his name: Only People Who've Published Something Matter.

Yes, that was the insidious, depressing, useless rule I had set for myself, as have many writers. I hated that rule the longer I lived with it as a companion. I hated it because, when all the writing dust settled, when I wasn't actively worrying about acceptance and rejection, or agents and editors, I actually felt like I mattered. My life mattered. It had to. It had to matter that I got up in the morning, and it had to matter when I kissed my wife, and it had to matter when I played with my children, and it had to matter when I wrote something even if I didn't publish it. Every choice I made had to matter, because making them felt important. I knew the difference between choosing something I loved and something I didn't. I knew the difference between liking something and not liking something, between being bored and being entertained, between being excited and disinterested. I knew the difference and it had to goddamn matter—because if *that* didn't matter, what did?

It's a good question, but one I couldn't really answer when it came to writing because when it came to writing I seemed to want clear evidence that my work and I mattered. Once I had been published, I was able to see the obvious cruelty and dis-honesty of my rule. Not only could I not apply it to all the as-piring writers I met at the conference, I also knew that I would not have been able to publish that book if all the choices I had made along my writing journey hadn't mattered.

Such is the transformative teaching capacity of experi-ence. As I wandered through the conference that day, I was reminded of stories of people who'd been raised in small, iso-lated, conservative towns and been taught to fear certain groups of people who didn't live in that community. Then someone leaves the town, moves to a city, and meets all the kinds of people they were supposed to be afraid of, all the people who were to be avoided because they're supposed to be so unknowably different. Sometimes people hang on to their biases out of tribal loyalty, just as I hung on to my rule, to my companion, for a long time despite disliking it. More often, however, experience wins out over habit. If someone tells you a certain kind of person is totally different from you, is utterly unapproachable, and then you meet that kind of person and they aren't, which should you believe—a story about that per-son, or your experience of the person? If you can't trust your *own* experience, what can you trust?

If you want to enjoy your whole writing journey, from its quiet, private beginnings to all the noisy, public stops along the way, you must have a clear understanding of success: what it actually is and what it can never be. And that understanding begins and ends with experience.

First, let's look at what success *isn't*. My friend Laura spent fifteen years writing and not selling novels. Then she sold a piece to the Modern Love column in the *New York Times* that received so many hits it temporarily shut down the *Times's* website. She had a publishing contract for her memoir the next day. When I met Laura for coffee shortly after her first whirlwind book tour, she greeted me with a huge smile. "I figured it out, Bill. Success doesn't exist!"

She had just been to the Miami Book Fair, where she'd found herself in the company of lots of established, "successful" writers. One of those authors was a man who'd published six literary novels, all of which had sold well. He'd published short stories in the *New Yorker, Harper's*, the *Paris Review*, and many other prestigious literary journals. He was doing well enough that he didn't need to supplement his income with teaching if he didn't want to. For a writer of literary fiction, he was having, by all accounts, a successful career. And yet he told Laura that he felt like a failure.

Why? Because he hadn't won the National Book Award.

"Can you *believe* it?" she asked.

Yes, I thought. *I can.*

It is so tempting to create a knowable, definitive, and yet ultimately arbitrary destination we call success. Writing is full of these destinations. You either have an agent or you don't. You've either published a story in a literary magazine or you haven't. You've either been on the *New York Times* bestsellers list or you haven't. That is to say: You've either arrived or you haven't. How nice to know where you are. How nice to know you *are* a success.

Nice, except just like all the boundaries and borders we've

drawn on our maps, these destinations are entirely invented. What you call success may not be what I call it. What's more, what I call success today I may not call success tomorrow. I know a man whose third novel spent three years on the best-seller list. Three years! Yet the book always hovered around number four or five. I was talking to him one day, and he said, "The book's still doing well, but how can I get it to number *one*?" The mind invents new destinations, new rules, new boundaries. But just as the earth does not recognize our man-made borders, doesn't grow flowers on one side and not the other, doesn't rain on one side and not the other, so too the reality of experience does not recognize our definitions of success any more than it recognizes our fears and biases.

So, what *is* success? You need look no further than the everyday experience of writing itself. Every single book—whether it sells no copies, a thousand copies, or a million copies—is written in precisely the same way: one word at a time. It's the only way to do it. The experience of finding the right word, or the right sentence, or the right story that you—not me, not Stephen King, not Margaret Atwood, but *you*—most want to tell is always satisfying. If you're a writer, you've had this experience many times. It's what's kept you writing, that feeling of finding something that is both new and familiar, finding the word that drops into a sentence like the right piece into a puzzle. In that moment, life itself makes sense. You are where you're supposed to be, doing what you're supposed to be doing.

I don't need to know you, or the kinds of stories you most

want to tell, to know that is true. It's true for all the writers that
have ever written. Our stories may be different, and our loopy,
useless definitions of external success may be different, but
the experience of successfully finding that right word has
been the same for as long as words and stories have existed. It's
the same because it's the reality of how a sentence and a scene
and a story is found. And while we can deny reality, or try to
invent reality, we can't escape reality. It's with us always, despite all our best efforts to define it for ourselves.

Success is not a destination but an experience. Period. It is
an experience because your *life* is not a destination but an
experience. When we dream of these successful destinations, whether it's a book contract or
winning the Pulitzer Prize or marry-
ing the perfect mate, we are almost always only imagining some transitional
experience beyond which all our experiences will be free of failure's haunting question: Am I good enough? For
some people marriage is proof they're
lovable; for some writers a publishing
contract is proof they're talented. We all have our rules. And
all those rules are a form of rejection, which every writer fears
and loathes.

Success is not a destination but an experience.

To place our happiness, our sense of well-being, somewhere out in an ever-distant future is to hold ourselves hos-
tage, to declare that these experiences I am having *now* are
not as valuable as the experience I might someday know. To
think this way is to reject the value of your very life, the way

an editor might reject a story, to tell yourself: This is not interesting. This is not worthy of my full attention.

And if you're writer, you live for acceptance in some way. Practically speaking, you must. You can't have a writing career without it. Someone out there has to like your stuff, from agents, to editors, to reviewers, to readers. That acceptance from others is an experience that begins at home. The *only* way to write a story that will find a publisher or a readership is for the writer to first value the experience of writing that story, to value the experience of discovering the idea, and of giving that idea shape, of finding the right words and removing the wrong ones. If the writer does not accept that this experience matters, that it is worthy of his full attention, then he will not find the full story. Instead, he'll offer up some half-written, pre-rejected version of it.

In other words, you must first decide an experience you enjoy, you find interesting, you find meaningful, is valuable simply because you find it interesting and meaningful. I thought of this when I interviewed Willy Vlautin. Willy's an extremely humble guy who, as of this writing, is the author of five well-reviewed novels, one of which, *Lean on Pete*, was made into a film. We got to talking about being an author, about book tours and publishers and reviews and such. "I don't really know about all that stuff, man," he said. "I'm just glad they keep publishing my stuff. I'm just glad I get to keep doing this."

This seemed to me to be the perfect strategy for any successful career. To say to yourself, "I love doing this. How can I do more of it?" As soon as you've identified something you love doing, the most natural next thought is about doing more of it. It's why we're on the planet. To find what we love to do and do it as often as we can, to follow it where it wants to go, to let it change and grow as it must so that it remains as interesting as when we first discovered it. My mind can always answer this question: *How can I do more of what I love?* because the answer is always the next step. If I have an idea for a story, and I like that idea, but my first thought is, *Where will I publish it?* my mind probably won't know the answer because publishing is not the next step. That is many, many steps away. Before I get there, I must find that story's first sentence. That's enough. Then the next sentence. And on and on and on. My mind is good at finding what comes next; it stinks at predicting the future.

As does everyone's. The future is none of my business. The next step is my business. I know this based on how much time I've spent thinking about the future. I build it and build it and build it in my imagination. Then that future collapses as soon as I return my attention to the present moment, to reality, to where I actually live. The present moment is where I experience everything. And if I do not know how to enjoy that present moment, absorb that present moment, I will not know how to enjoy and absorb it in the future when I have achieved that which I believe is worthy of being enjoyed and absorbed. I'll get there, and my fretful mind will already be leaping ahead to a new future, for that is what I've trained it to do.

We writers must practice bringing our attention to the present moment, to the blank page, to the story that wants to be told. Someday, riches and acclaim may be yours, if they aren't already. But today, the page is waiting for you. Today, the experience of finding your story is waiting for you. It is right there with you, a loyal and friendly companion who'll be with you from beginning to end.

CHAPTER FOUR

The Practice

I was sitting on my couch stewing in the disappointment from another rejection letter. I was four books into my novel-writing noncareer and these letters were virtually all I'd known. Usually I threw the letters away and tried to move on as quickly as possible. But on that afternoon I was feeling reflective. *What's going on?* I asked myself.

Normally when I asked this sort of question, I didn't expect an answer. It wasn't really a question. It was just another way of complaining. Sometimes, however, having grown exhausted from fruitless complaint, I directed the question toward myself and listened for an actual answer, which is exactly what I got that day.

*You'll never publish anything—*I heard—*until you straighten this out.*

As is always the case, whatever spoke to me that afternoon did so in a language in which I was uniquely fluent. That is to say, I knew precisely what it was that needed straightening out. I could not yet name it—which was that everyone has what it takes—but I could feel it. I could feel my resistance to it, could feel its constant presence in my life, and I was *not* happy that this was the answer I'd received. To address it, I felt, would mean straightening out my entire life.

That's not fair, I thought in reply. *Why should I have to reach enlightenment just to publish a damn book? Hemingway didn't. He was a drunk and a philanderer. Emily Dickinson was a shut-in. David Bowie was strung out for the first half of his career. Beethoven was an asshole. Why do I have to be perfect?*

I was back to complaining, which meant I had no intention of straightening anything out just then. I wanted what I wanted and I didn't want to do anything differently to get it. But I had my own attention, and though I dug in and plowed ahead as I'd been doing before, I would not be able to avoid this forever, any more than I could avoid aging or hair loss.

I would eventually learn why it was that I, in particular, had to learn that everyone has what it takes, and why I thought this meant that I had to be perfect, which I'll address in chapter 5 (skip ahead if you'd like). But I had noticed something that day that you may have noticed as well. Namely, if accepting that everyone has what it takes is the key to full success, why do so many people have success without accepting they have what it takes? For that matter, why do so many artists, specifically, make such beautiful stuff while leading such screwy, self-destructive, abusive, chaotic lives?

The answer, quite simply, is: They work around it. This is what we all do. The way I worked around it was that sometimes

I'd sit down to write, and if I let myself sink into the dream of the story I was telling, if I forgot to care what anyone would think of it, if I forgot to wonder if I had what it took, if I didn't try to measure the quality of every sentence I'd just written but only tried to find the best next sentence, there was no problem at all. There was only the story unfolding, and the characters doing what characters do, and the electric thrill of discovery. When I forgot to compare myself or measure myself or judge myself, I wrote as well as I could write that day, and I felt happy. I felt confident. And I didn't worry about the future or myself or my talent because I couldn't feel better or clearer or more on purpose than that.

But it didn't always go that well. Sometimes I'd sit down to write and I *would* wonder if I had what it took, and I would wonder what people would think about me, and I would look at each sentence and think, *Is that the kind of sentence a good writer would write?* Whenever this happened, there were lots of problems. Nothing went well or came easily. Nothing I wrote—if I wrote at all—surprised me. I felt like a fraud. I hated my story and I hated my life and I hated myself. I'd get up from the desk despondent, hopeless, and grit my way through the rest of my day, doing all I could to ignore the nagging feeling of hopelessness until I found myself back at the desk the next day where I prayed that by some gift of the capricious Muse it would go well and I could like myself and my life again.

Regardless of whether my writing went well, I still had to live all those hours away from my desk *not* writing, and those were some of the most dangerous hours in the day. When you're not writing, you can think anything at all about what you have written or will write. And if you've not published anything yet, the kinds of things you think can get pretty gloomy pretty easily.

So, I lived day to day with gloominess and uncertainty as well as spikes of hope and enthusiasm. I accepted that this was what life was like, the way I accepted the changes in the weather, enduring the rain and snow, enjoying the sun and warmth, because what else can you do? I accepted it, but I believed that one day, one day when I'd published a book or two, one day when I was making more money, one day when the good reviews had poured in, all this would be different and I would not wake up every day wondering whether it was heaven or hell that awaited me.

That's how I worked around the reality I could feel but could not accept. I accepted and endured unhappiness and uncertainty, I drank more wine than I should have some nights, and I got used to waking up in the middle of the night in a nameless terror. I complained to my wife, I lost my temper with my kids, and I played too many video games. That's how I avoided and worked around it and got by. That's how most people do, more or less. You can live a whole life that way. You can sell a million books and live in a house on the hill that way. It can be done. People can endure a saga's worth of suffering. We're brilliant at it.

But it's not necessary. That everyone has what it takes means that, regardless of income or age or strength or looks, everyone is inherently, unequivocally, nonnegotiably equal. Everyone, top to bottom, for all of time. This is much easier to think or write or say than it is to live. It's not so easy to wander around the world and think no one's better than you because they have better hair or a better car or have sold more books or have all their limbs or are laughing when you're crying. And it's not so easy to think no one's worse because they're yelling at their kid or their clothes don't fit or they're panhandling or they're cheating. Sometimes seeing a world where everyone has what it takes feels like learning to walk a tightrope, needing the handhold of knowing who I am better than or worse than just to know where I stand.

Which is why knowing that you have what it takes because everyone has what it takes isn't an understanding; it's a practice. Like anything, the more you practice it, the easier it gets, but practice you must, always and forever. Equality is what you see when you look at life through the lens of love and acceptance, but that lens must be chosen again and again, must be chosen even when it appears dangerous or naïve. It is the only way to know the truth, to know yourself and other people.

So, how do you practice? Let's begin with writing itself, specifically what *other* people write, because reading other people's stuff is where most of the division occurs in our minds. There may be stories you read that you call "brilliant" or "a work of pure genius" or "perfect." You'll find the writing so good it'll intimidate you, and you might place that author in a special category of writers you believe are not just better than you but possess some magic quality known by only a lucky and gifted few. Theirs are the shining gems bright enough to be seen from the hilltop on which they reside.

Whereas, by comparison, you can only light some small corner of the ordinary world.

Likewise, you'll read stories you don't just dislike but you *disdain*: stories that seem sloppy and obvious and boring, stories that seem to describe life as you have never led it. You may be tempted to put the authors of these stories in yet another special category: the talentless and the ungifted. The stories these poor people write don't shine at all, they light no path for the reader, they only reveal the author's smallness and nearsightedness. It's a little embarrassing.

Both of these special categories are products of the same lie that some are better and some are worse. I have learned that no matter how much I like or dislike a story I read, I cannot judge its author. It disrupts my own writing. If there is such a thing as better or worse, my choice is that I simply *must* be better. Yet it's impossible to know if I am.

I have had to replace judgment with learning. What I like or dislike may not be the same sorts of things you like or dislike. What does or does not light me up, what I find compelling and what I find boring and obvious, is a form of guidance. I am seeing in other people's work what I would like to either see more of or less of in my work. That is all. The degree to which I like or dislike something is a reflection of how close or far a story is from the writing path I want to follow.

Thus, practically speaking, when I read something I like, I take note of why I liked it, what the author did linguistically or narratively that I found so effective or compelling. Perhaps it's similar to something I like to do and it serves to remind me why. Or if it's something I haven't tried yet, I file it away and might try it later. If I *don't* like what I've read, I take note of that as well. I might wonder how I would do it differently, or I might just think, *Let's never do that.*

More important, however, is to *own* my response to whatever I'm reading. Though it is tempting to think, *That's a good story,* or, *That story stinks,* what I really mean is, "I like that story," or, "I don't like that story." The second assessment is absolutely, unassailably true; the first is not. To think a story is good or is bad is to assume everyone on Earth would have the same response to it, the same as everyone on Earth would be cold in winter and hot in summer. If you are like me, you have read stories you love so much you can't imagine someone else not loving that story, and you have read stories you so dislike you can't imagine someone loving them. And yet if we take a moment, we know the truth. What you like and dislike is yours and yours alone. Own it.

When we view what we read in this way, all stories are helping all writers in one way or another. We are not here to all learn how to write the same story. We are here to learn how to write our story and only we can possibly know what that story is.

That's how I practice when I read. Of course, I forget the practice sometimes, get a little sloppy, and elevate or diminish a piece of work. That's okay. This error does not inflict a mortal wound to my creative soul. If I am paying attention, I will notice the mistake immediately, based on how grumpy and defensive I feel. If I am *not* paying attention, it will take me a little longer, and I will have to get that much more grumpy and miserable before I notice what's happening. No matter. In the end the result is the same. I return to my normal, in-the-moment self—unharmed and having learned a little bit more.

The practice doesn't end with reading, of course. It extends to every person I meet or see or learn about, whether they're writers or lawyers or children playing in the park. It extends to corrupt politicians and bank robbers and pirates. It extends to people I know and people I don't know, people I pass on the street and people who knock on my door. If equality does not extend to everyone, it's not equality. And so, I must practice it with other people. Here are a few examples of how I've learned to do that.

I attended my first writers' conference when I was thirty. I was looking forward to the experience, but I was bit intimidated as well. I would be pitching my first novel to a literary agent. I had never met an actual literary agent, and so I began imagining the woman to whom I had chosen to pitch like a cartoonish television villain. I worried she wouldn't like my book. In my imagination, she rose up from her chair, all designer clothes and rattling jewelry, and said, "Why are you *wasting* my time with this?" Oh, this made me mad. "I *paid* for this conference!" I replied—again, in my imagination. "I'm here because I love to write and share stories with people and it's *not* a waste of time." I was ready for her.

The day of the pitch came, and I went to my assigned spot in the hotel to wait my turn. Each agent had their own room and, from my perch of worry and doubt, I could see her through a window, shuffling around, getting herself some coffee. My appointed time arrived. I went in and shook her hand and introduced myself and she asked me to take a seat. She was a petite woman with stylish short hair and a very polite disposition. I gave my memorized pitch. She listened and nodded. Once it was clear she was not going to ask me why I was wasting her time, I began free-forming, talking about why I liked the book, about all the cool parts of it. She nodded and listened and said it sounded interesting.

Now that I wasn't scared of her, now that she wasn't a villain, I realized I was talking to someone who liked stories and literature as much as I did. I mentioned a very popular book I'd just read with which I'd had some serious gripes. She agreed with me the author had allowed his desire to be a Great Writer get in the way of his story. She told me that she thought literary writers could sell more books now that trade paperbacks were coming into fashion. That was that. She asked me to send the manuscript and I said I would. She did not end up representing me, but that was the first and last time I'd turn agents or editors into cartoon villains. They were just people who decided to make their living selling stories.

Many years later I had begun shooting video interviews with writers for *Author* magazine. I interviewed writers of all genres, most of whom I'd never heard of. Occasionally, however, I'd interview someone I considered famous. Such was the case when I sat down with Henry Winkler. Having grown up in the seventies, I'd been a fan of *Happy Days* and, like everyone I knew, thought Arthur Fonzarelli, *The Fonz*, was cool. He was an icon of my childhood. In fact, he was the very person who really introduced me to that iconic word—*cool*—and whenever I heard it, I'd picture The Fonz and his effortless confidence. There were other icons of my childhood—Farrah

Fawcett, the quarterback Ken Stabler, John Travolta—but I've never met any of them. Now here I was, shaking Henry Winkler's hand and thanking him for agreeing to the interview.

Of course, he was much older, a little pudgier, a lot grayer, and he was wearing a comfy green sweater and not The Fonz's black leather jacket and white T-shirt. He also wouldn't make lasting eye contact at first. Normally, the writers I interviewed were not used to being on camera and were excited and nervous and eager to chat as we prepared for the interview. But once Winkler and I were seated, and my cameraman began arranging the lights and checking the sound, he looked everywhere but at me. I began to feel unseen and unimportant, as if I was still watching this man on television, just one of millions, while he was one of a kind.

This was no good. I knew I couldn't interview him feeling this way, so I reminded myself that maybe he was so used to being interviewed that he'd learned that he had to keep some sense of privacy to save his energy until the cameras were rolling. This helped, but I could still feel that difference I'd created in my mind between him and me, between celebrity and noncelebrity. *Ignore it,* I told myself. *Ignore it even though it feels real.*

Sure enough, as soon as we began filming, as soon as I asked him my first question, he gave me his full attention, and we were talking about his Hank Zipzer series, his young adult books about a boy with dyslexia. Winkler himself has dyslexia. He told me that all his life he'd secretly believed he was dumb, that he'd been trying to navigate this deficiency; it wasn't until he began publishing these books that he decided maybe he *was* smart. I then told him about my son and his challenges with school, and Henry Winkler turned to the camera and spoke directly to Jack, telling him he shouldn't worry, that he'd learn, that there was nothing wrong with him.

By the time the interview was over, I could not see the icon anymore; he'd been replaced by a person with vulnerabilities and desires and ideas and compassion. I liked him. When he got up to leave, he shook my hand. "Thanks," he said. "That was different." I was glad to hear that. It wouldn't have been a different interview unless I'd let myself talk to him author-to-author, father-to-father, person-to-person, rather than fan-to-celebrity. In short, I'd let myself be myself. I never feel like myself when I think the person I'm talking to is better than me, is somehow more deserving of attention than I am. When I believe in this difference, I feel like a peasant trying to figure out how to behave in the presence of the king.

Years later I decided I wanted to do more public speaking. A friend of mine who was a professional speaker told me I should talk to Rotary Clubs.

"Rotary Clubs?" I said. "They still exist?"

"They most certainly do," she said.

There were tons of them, in fact, and they were always looking for speakers. Fair enough, I thought, and I drafted my speech proposals, sent them off to the clubs around Seattle, and soon I had five gigs lined up. Success!

On the day of the first talk, I made my way to the restaurant where the chapter met. I arrived just as the chapter president was setting up for the meeting. He was a large, genial man who described his organization as "a bunch of do-gooders." I liked do-gooders, but I began to get a funny feeling about the gig. The president had brought his own American flag for the event. I liked America, but I was not so keen on flags. I am instinctively not a joiner, and there is something about a flag that to me says, "You're either with us, or against us." The Rotarians began filing in and taking their seats. They were all very nice, but each time they asked me about myself and I told them I was writer, they got an odd look in their eyes, as if they were meeting a new species.

I don't belong here, I thought. *These aren't my people.* I didn't despise them, but they seemed too conservative, a little too businessy, and their niceness seemed largely a function of not wanting to upset the order of things. And then, as the meeting was called to order, the president stood, turned to the flag, put his hand over his heart, and announced, "Let's begin with the Pledge of Allegiance."

I panicked a little. I hadn't said the Pledge of Allegiance since I was in fifth grade. I didn't realize until that moment that I wasn't a fan. It smacked of indoctrination. But everyone in that room, man and woman, young and old, was facing the flag, hand over heart. Much as I wanted to, I couldn't sit this one out. As a man who was about to take the mic, I didn't feel it would be wise to alienate my audience. But this did little to soothe my discomfort. I said the pledge, all the while thinking, *I'm not one of them. This is a very bad idea.*

Then it was time to speak. My talk that afternoon was

called "No One Is Broken," about that valuable lesson I learned raising Jack. I stood behind the lectern, a few steps from the flag, and looked out at their politely waiting faces. *Well, I'll just do this,* I thought, *and whatever happens, happens.* I had done enough theater and public speaking to know that once you start, you can feel the audience, you can see the audience, but you can't focus on the audience. You can't think about them and what they might be thinking about you. Whether I thought they were friendly or unfriendly, all my attention had to be on the stories I was telling.

And that's what I did. I forgot about the American flag, the writers and nonwriters, the conservatives and liberals, and remembered instead why no one was broken, and how that had changed my view of myself and other people. If you're a writer, you know this experience. When we write we forget about everything but the story we're telling. We forget about the world outside our windows as we slip completely into that dream. In that lovely time, the story is more real to us than the outside world's troubles and traumas. This is what it can be like with public speaking if you let it, which I did that day.

I slipped into the stories. And as is always the case, I had little awareness of the passage of time until I had reached the end. I had been enjoying myself, you see. I love telling stories, I love using words to spin this virtual reality in which we can all share, and I love that stories ask us to focus on what is so meaningful and moving about life. When I was done, folks clapped, I thanked them, and went to gather my stuff.

Rotarians began coming up to me, telling me about their

grandchild or niece or cousin who were on the spectrum. Another told me he had always wanted to write, and that he felt his life would make a great book. Still another just said, "No one is broken. Huh. I'm going to think about that." Driving home, I thought, *Well, that wasn't such a bad idea after all.*

This cycle repeated itself at each of the next four gigs. I'd arrive at the restaurant or club where we were meeting, look around at the Rotarians and think, *This is a bad idea.* Then I would give my talk, have a few lovely conversations afterward, sell a couple books even, and drive home thinking, *That went fine.* It was like I was solving the same riddle again and again.

This is how I practice seeing a world where everyone has what it takes. Beyond the veil of labels—agent, celebrity, businessman, conservative, liberal, writer—is a person finding their way through the world. The labels can be acquired and discarded like clothing as our paths change: Once I called myself a novelist; now I call myself a teacher. Businessmen become dancers, dancers become entrepreneurs. I can't relate to someone's label or their race or their gender or their political leanings. I can only relate to their humanity, to that curious, tender focus of attention guided ultimately by love. Sometimes I can't see past the veil; either it's too thick or I'm too intimidated by the person or think I need something from the person. Sometimes I only see the person on TV or on the Internet and, lacking that immediate energetic connection that only comes face-to-face, I turn them into heroes or villains, something slightly more or less than I.

It doesn't matter. The veil is the veil is the veil. That I cannot see beyond it does not change what it obscures. If I cannot see beyond it in others, I turn my attention inward and try to see in myself what I cannot see in someone else. I turn my attention in and remember who I am before writer, before teacher, before father or husband. I turn my attention in to the same naked self that would love as it wants to be loved.

CHAPTER FIVE

Good Questions

When I was three years old, my mother, father, older sister, and I played a little game of football in our living room. The big green rug that stretched from corner to corner served as our playing field, and my mother and I were one team, and my father and sister another. On that afternoon, my father and sister were victorious—an outcome, I suspect, predetermined by some parental math. When my sister scored the last touchdown, and my father lifted her in the air in celebration, I collapsed onto the floor and began to weep.

My poor mother tried to console me: It was just a game; we'd play another; did I want some cookies? The cookies were a good idea, but hardly a substitute for what I believed I had been deprived of at the game's end. I had lost, which meant I did not have what the winners had, which had to be something good or else why want it in the first place? Since I didn't have it, I had less, and less was always worse than more, and so my life, in some small measurable way, was worse than what it might have been had I won. And if not, what was the point of it all in first place?

Did I think those actual words in my three-year-old mind? I did not. But I did feel an unarticulated question in my heart, a question that had to be answered in some way or another: *Is there a difference between the winner and the loser?* My first answer was, "Yes." And so I cried because the answer was unbearable to me, but one I figured I'd just have to learn to live with.

That is my first memory. My life to that point—unless my parents managed to keep some dark secrets from me—was free of loss and trauma. No one I knew and loved had died or moved away. What's more, my younger brother, my older sister, my father, and, to some degree, my mother were all competitive. We all liked games, and we all played them to win. And yet I was the only bad loser in the group. I was the only one who pouted and fumed, who threw chairs and flipped Monopoly boards. It was as if I'd arrived on Earth with that question about winning and losing, about having and not having, ripe and ready in my mind—and I would spend the rest of my life answering it.

I don't think I'm unusual in this way. The only difference— though I don't consider it a meaningful one—between me and most of the writers I know is that my question is not tied to some formative life experience. Instead, my question seemed to *lead me* to life experiences over and over and over again— from games and races I'd win and lose, to girlfriends I had and lost, to a writing career defined by acceptance (winning) and rejection (losing)—each of which brought the question forward again. Most of what I have called suffering and relief in my life has been the consequence of how I answered in a given moment.

On the other hand, many of the writers I've met at conferences or through interviews, or whom I've taught in workshops or coached as clients, are learning to answer questions that seem to have grown out of an experience or circumstance in their childhood. Often these are dramatic: poverty, abuse, violence, death, disease. I say "seem" because I wonder if we all arrive with some question in our hearts. And while I first heard mine in a family game of football on a big green rug, and another first heard hers when her family was homeless, the consequence is the same: If we answer the question incorrectly, if our answer is different from Life's answer—which is always kind and always forgiving and always accepting and always inclusive—we will suffer and struggle around our misunderstanding, building lives on an unstable and unsustainable belief.

If you are the type of person who likes to write, those questions will send you to the page. Writing, remember, is driven by questions: *What do I want to write about today? What does my hero do for a living? What is my heroine's weakness? What's the best word?* Most of what I do when I write is ask questions and wait for answers. If I don't like the answers I get, I ask my question differently. The better the question, the

> *The better the question, the better the answer.*

better the answer. What we call *craft* is, in many ways, learning which questions to ask and which questions not to ask.

Craft can be fun for writers because we are aware that we are choosing the questions. It is also why we can teach some aspects of craft. For instance, many beginning memoirists fall into the trap of *telling* the reader about their lives rather than *showing* them specific scenes illustrating that life. I did this myself when I first moved from fiction to creative nonfiction. I knew certain things were true about my childhood—that I was a romantic, that I didn't want to fight other boys, that I enjoyed daydreaming—and that these inclinations were somehow all branches off the same tree. So, I'd write pages and pages, articulately *explaining* about the effortlessness of love, and the effort it takes to hit someone, and how the imagination always moves in the most effortless direction. Then I'd reread what I'd written and think, *That's all true. I wonder if there are a few actual events, actual scenes, I could depict that would show the exact same thing so the reader could make this connection themselves?* This happened again and again. I'd explain and then I'd look for a scene, explain and look for scene, until, finally, I started looking for a scene first. I'd learned the right question to ask.

Craft applies to every kind of story. No matter what you write, nouns and verbs will be more effective than adjectives and adverbs, clichés will feel stale and lifeless, and dialogue will sound more authentic when characters don't say exactly what they're thinking. I can appreciate craft in every story I read or watch the way I've heard professional athletes praise other athletes. Sometimes you have to do something regularly to understand how difficult it is to even begin to master it, how what appears natural and effortless from the outside is actually an expression of hours of practice. As a storyteller, I appreciate storytelling skill, as well as the discipline I know was necessary to acquire that skill.

What is not always so easy to appreciate, however, are the questions that drive a storyteller to the page in the first place. Unlike the craft questions we choose, these other questions seem to be chosen for us. In almost every case, we are not even aware we are asking them. Even now, as I sit here choosing to write this book about creativity and self-doubt, about having and not having, the question I first heard back when I was three continues to compel me forward silently. Even now I find myself drawn to tell stories in this book for reasons I do not fully understand until I am done telling them and I feel that relief of discovery. The question about the difference between the winner and the loser I'd forgotten I was asking answered once again.

I fool myself every day into believing I've answered it once and for all. How could I not? I've been writing about it every day for the last ten years or so, to more or less the exclusion of everything else. I didn't know it was what I was writing about back when I started, but it was. And yet I am still surprised by my answers, still excited by the search, as each answer reveals another facet of the question.

I am not unique at all in this unfolding, though I did not fully understand what I shared with other writers until I began interviewing them. For the last ten years, I've rarely read a book unless I'm going to meet or at least talk to its author.

This was not the case for the first forty-three years of my life. In fact, until I started the magazine, I had never met the author of anything I'd read; I'd never even gone to a book signing.

In those days, authors were not real people to me. They were names attached to stories. Whether I liked a story determined what I thought of the person who'd written it. I had very low opinions of people who wrote stories I didn't like. When I tried to picture who they were, all that came to mind was the part of the story that bothered me so much. If I found a story pretentious, in my imagination its author took every single thing they did much too seriously. If I found a story's ending unnecessarily grim, in my imagination its author never smiled, never laughed, never rejoiced.

Then I interviewed Jane, a romance writer. Though I had read a lot of fantasy novels when I was a young teen, by the time I entered college I read only what is considered literary fiction. It's also what I wrote. I had never read a romance novel in my life until interviewing Jane, though I had seen their covers in the wire racks in grocery stores and had drawn my conclusions about their contents. I believed that to succeed as a literary writer I had to abide by certain rules. Stories could not be even slightly sentimental; the language had to be original, concise, and true; characters were expected to behave exactly like real people; and the stories absolutely could not have tidy, easy, happy endings because if you've actually lived an adult life you know that's *not* how things go. Romance writers, I believed, broke all these rules. The covers spoke to me of a fantasy view of love and even life itself. These kinds of fantasies were for kids. What were grown-ups doing reading and writing such things?

Because Jane was a Seattle author, we had arranged to shoot the interview at her home. We found a well-lit corner of her house and started the interview. She told me how she had written fourteen novels before she sold anything. It had been very hard writing all those books and selling nothing. Rejection after rejection after rejection. One day she finally asked herself if she wanted to quit, gave herself the actual option of giving it all up. She realized then that it didn't matter. Whether she ever sold something or not, she would be writing for the rest of her life. A week later, she got her first acceptance letter from Harlequin.

She told me how she had written and published at least three romance books a year for almost a decade. *Three?* I asked. I didn't know then how common this pace was for romance writers. She still wrote romances because they helped to pay the bills, but now she was also writing contemporary women's fiction. "I love the romances," she said. "They're fairy tales. I see them like a gift to my readers. I like fairy tales, too. But life has darkness, you know? And in the fairy tales, you can't really get into the darkness, and I just had to write about it. I mean I *needed* to write about it, so that's why I'm writing these other books now also."

She told me bit about the darkness she'd known in her life, about her difficult childhood and her father's depression, about attending an MFA program and how some of the teachers and students treated the pretty young woman who wanted to write romance fiction. She told me about her divorce and raising two boys on her own and the uncertainty of money when you're a writer. We finished the interview by going up into her study, where she showed me her story maps, the large corkboard where she laid out her plot and kept track of her characters.

Driving home from Jane's, I thought of all the books I had written and hadn't published. It was a lot less than fourteen. I remembered how I had once stood in the middle of a restaurant I was working in and asked myself if I still wanted to write. I decided I needed to let the answer be "No" if that's what it would be, and how in that moment I saw my thirteen-year-old self writing his first novel at his typewriter before school, and I thought, *What would you tell him if you quit?*

And I thought about all the times darkness had come to visit me in my bed in the middle of the night or on drives home from the restaurant. It's hell on earth when you're in it, when nothing seems worth doing, when everything you've done seems to have come to nothing. To be in such a place is to forget why life is worth living. There is no right way or wrong way out of that hell. If writing a romance novel lights the way back to life, I thought, then by God, write that romance novel.

I began pounding on my steering wheel. "That's right!" I said to no one at all. "Write the damn romance novel. Write them all!" I hadn't felt that good in a while. How nice to be free at last of the idea that some stories shouldn't be told. Believing a story shouldn't be told is like believing a life shouldn't be lived.

A few years later I interviewed novelist Jerry Stahl, who,

after his career in magazine and television writing went a bit south, became hooked on heroin and found himself working at McDonald's. He managed to claw his way out of *that* hell and eventually wrote the memoir *Permanent Midnight*, which was made into a movie. We had a great conversation about his latest novel and about addiction and about the redemptive nature of creativity. In the middle of the interview, he said, "Man, you sound like you've *really* been through it!"

"I've never been addicted to anything," I said, "but I've definitely been through it in my own way."

"I know, man," he said. "I can tell."

I think sometimes of Jane and Jerry and me, and all the writers I've known who've found themselves in hell and have had to climb their way out. How different those paths must look from the outside, but how similar hell is when you're there. The despair of hopelessness, of joylessness, has no real shape. It flattens life, making all choices seem equally irrelevant. Nothing matters. Nothing will change anything. Nothing works.

Do you know where there is also nothing? The blank page. What a perfectly clean starting place. My page is as blank as your page is as blank as Jerry's and Jane's and Shakespeare's, too. It's where everything begins. When you sit down to that page, that inviting, empty space, you must make room in your heart for every story that might be told. You'll only tell one that day, but first you make room for them all. The question your life has been asking you pulses on, whether you hear it in your mind or not. Your misery, your hell, was an invention of your mind, when you tried to answer that question without love. Now you're looking for the real answer, for Life's answer, and you will only hear it when you let whatever it must be come. Let it be romance or literature, steampunk or poetry. It doesn't matter. It's not for you to decide. The answer is always simpler than you imagined in your fevered dreams of despair, the same way the best stories you will ever tell seem to write themselves.

CHAPTER SIX

Connection

This is how it used to go for me: Sometimes I'd sit down to write and I'd fall into the dream of the story I was telling and it was like I'd become caught in its current. That current was going somewhere, often somewhere fast, and my job was not really to tell the story but to keep up with it, to stay in its center where the movement was swiftest and straightest. When I was writing fiction, the characters would say surprising things, things I could never have planned for them. It was as if I was listening to them, not writing them. The world those characters inhabited looked as real to me as my own, and I did my best to accurately describe it, as if I had traveled to a distant country and was reporting back on its mysteries and majesty for my readers. I wasn't making anything up. I was seeing and following and listening. When it was going really well, the experience was absolutely effortless.

Those were the best days. When I was done writing, I

didn't care whether what I'd written would be published or not. All I cared about was how I felt as I pushed away from my desk. If I didn't start congratulating myself, or imagining what reviewers would say, I felt as if I was still in that current even though I wasn't telling a story. I didn't want anything or need anything. Any regrets that might have haunted me the day before seemed no more real than monsters that had chased me in a previous night's sleep. I was at peace.

Other times it didn't go so well. I couldn't find whatever door in my imagination I'd fallen through when I'd become happily lost in the story. I'd write anyway. Nothing was easy. I would beg my characters to do something interesting and they'd stare back at me, mannequins with dead eyes. I'd become impatient and give them commands, which they would clumsily obey like actors with no enthusiasm for their roles. When I turned my attention to the world these cheap golems inhabited, it was like I was seeing old photographs of a place for which I'd lost all fondness. I'd slog on like this for as long as I could bear it, feeling like a talentless fraud until I'd give up and walk away, hating the story, hating my life, hating myself.

There were lots of days that were in between this. I'd drift in and out of that current, never sure what allowed me in or punted me out. So it went, I believed. Such was the writing life. After many years like this, the bad days seemed to get worse and worse. My tolerance for the hopelessness that followed me thinned. The emptiness of it felt like a wound I reopened every time I shoved away from the desk in frustration.

Pain can be helpful in this way. Sometimes it is the only means by which I will change. By and by I noticed that how quickly I got into that current, that flow, depended on how curious and interested I was in the story I was telling. How long I stayed in The Flow depended on whether I wondered what other people would think of what I was writing. The Flow was mercilessly consistent. I had to be authentically, personally interested and I couldn't for one moment care whether anyone else would be interested. These rules were absolute. I know because I tried breaking them, sometimes out of old habit, sometimes out of a kind of rebellion.

I rarely break the rules anymore. I'm a slow learner sometimes but a learner nonetheless. The more time I spend in The Flow, the more I learn about it. The first thing I learned was that when I'm in it, I feel wholly a part of something for which I am not wholly responsible. The Flow exists before and after I am in it. I can't take credit for it; at most, I am responsible for getting into it. As such, it is also equally available to everybody. When I'm writing in The Flow, I'm tapped into something universal, like a computer is connected to the Internet.

I don't know how else to describe the experience. It's why for a long time I only liked talking to other writers about it. I disliked the incredulity I'd sometimes encounter when I'd bring it up at a party. To be clear, you don't have to write to get in it. I've been in The Flow when exercising or having a conversation or going shopping. It's just that I'm most acutely aware of it when I'm writing because it is *impossible* to write when I'm not in it. I can easily shop, talk, or exercise when I'm out of The Flow. I may not enjoy doing any of those things, but I can still do them. When I'm trying to write when I'm out of The Flow, it's like I've forgotten what a story is, what a sentence is. I'm lost from word one.

Which is why I so disliked other people's incredulity when I talked about the magical nature of writing. When you're out of The Flow, you can forget what it's like to be in it. It doesn't take long to not only forget but to begin doubting The Flow was real in the first place. Then you start talking about it to someone else, maybe just to remind yourself, to bolster yourself, but you don't sound convincing because you're trying to convince yourself, and now their doubt is a reflection of your doubt. It's easy to hate those poor people then, those infidels, those nonbelievers. How absolutely alone I feel when out of The Flow, how disconnected from the source of everything good that has ever come into my life. As a writer, I may crave the solitude of my workspace, but I never want to be lonely.

I spent many years feeling lonely now and again and always believing the cure for that loneliness was other people. Sometimes it was, and sometimes it wasn't. Sometimes I'd feel lonely in a crowd, having no sense of my connection to anyone around me. Those strangers might as well all have been agents and editors, rejecting and rejecting and rejecting me. The worst loneliness, though, was when I was by myself, surrounded by nothing but dead furniture and joyless obligations. I felt obsolete, a soldier awaiting his orders at a post his commander had long abandoned. In those moments, my whole life was the like the emptiness of the page when I've lost track of the story.

I experienced this loneliness most acutely when I was a very young man, before I was married. I never experienced it so brutally once I was living with Jen, my wife. I attributed the change to marriage. We were both homebodies who liked hanging around with each other. Even when she was off at class or work, I could feel a sort of friendly ghost of her company in our apartment. If the writing went poorly, and I felt that dead fear of talentlessness like a stone in my heart, I could go to her, a writer herself, and moan about my miserable circumstance. She'd try to think of something to say to make me feel better, which every so often she did, but mostly I just wanted to be around her, to feel connected to someone and something again.

If I sound dramatic, I was. I was the sort of young man prone to ask, "What's the point of it all?" It seemed like a very important question. The idea of slogging blindly through life, marching toward some pointless, nameless, meaningless end was unbearable to me. The lower I felt, the more I asked myself that question.

Yet I never asked myself that supposedly important question when I had found a story and was chasing it. I never asked it when I was in a good conversation or watching a show I loved or reading a great book or playing some music. I never ever asked it when connected to The Flow. Whenever I was in The Flow, I felt as though I was exactly where I was supposed to be, doing exactly what I was supposed to be doing.

Which has led me to this final conclusion about The Flow. I have wanted many *things* in my life. I have wanted money, attention, sex, approval, a bigger house, a better car, a more lucrative contract. I've wanted those things, by and large, because of how I believed they would make feel when I had them. But I never felt better than when I was in The Flow. In truth, all I have ever wanted was the connection I feel while in it. As soon as I have that connection, my life makes sense.

Moreover, every *thing* I feel I want comes as a consequence of that connection, and nothing has taught me that more directly than writing. As I said, I can't write until I'm in The Flow. All the craft I've learned is useless to me when I'm out of The Flow. Once I'm in, I can employ the craft to shape what comes to me—but nothing comes to me if I'm disconnected. The connection is immeasurably more important than the skill. In fact, a beginning writer can produce something quite beautiful, quite skillful, if the connection is strong enough.

This relationship of connection and creation is an everyday practice. Every time I sit down to write, I must remember that it's connection first, writing second. Connection first. Writing second. The stories will come, the contracts will come, the sales will come, but only if and when I'm connected. Without the connection, nothing worth keeping or sharing ever comes.

My desire for connection does not end when I'm done writing. The difference, as I said, is that I can live my life, do my shopping, and mow the lawn, whether or not I feel connected. Then, of course, when I am disconnected, I feel irritable and dissatisfied. I begin wondering what I need to make me feel better. More money? More sales? A new deck? What I wanted is more connection. It's all I've ever wanted.

It's all anyone has ever wanted. That connection is one of

the most mysterious aspects of writing—specifically that we are all connected to the same font of inspiration. I can't prove this, of course, but I believe you can experience a sincere connection whether you think you are connected to something universal or something specific to you. I do think it will be easier for you to experience that connection if you accept that you're drawing from the same pool of inspiration as your neighbor, whether that neighbor writes or not.

Writers are notorious introverts. If you are like me, you must spend a certain amount of time alone every day to feel like yourself. I love teaching and being with people, but only in measured amounts. This need for solitude requires a mature understanding of loneliness. Loneliness is not a consequence of isolation but of disconnection. It is easy to believe the opposite because so often the company of other people, particularly our loved ones, has been such an easy and immediate means of that connection. But I have been in the company of my closest friends, my dearest family, and thought, *I need to find a door, get on the other side of it, and close it.*

I don't consider this impulse unfriendly in the least. Writing is inherently friendly. I can't share a story with an enemy. An enemy is someone utterly different from me. An enemy is someone who shares nothing with me, not his coat nor his hearth nor his values. He is a complete enigma who would reject anything lovely I might offer.

It is easy to begin seeing a friend as an enemy if I believe I am too special, that I possess a special connection to a special source of inspiration. How could someone not as special as I possibly understand me? How could they be my friend?

How could they possibly understand the value of what that special connection brought me if they do not possess that same connection? After all, everything *I've* ever read or heard or seen that I loved felt like a story or a song written somehow for me. The artist rendered something I had seen but forgotten, had experienced but had not properly valued. The artist showed me that value, showed me what I had possessed but had ignored.

If you want to share your stories with other people, if you want to be an author, you must accept that ultimately, everyone is just like you. All your stories are descriptions of what the universal connection brings you. You must trust that you're sharing something that belongs to everyone. That Flow, that connection, is a kind of universal language. Do not believe for a moment that you are speaking in some obscure form of tongues. You're not some oddity, some member of a small, exclusive club. You're one of us, writers and readers and bankers and bakers alike, and always have been.

After all, whether you write romance or science fiction or literary fiction or mysteries or poetry or superhero screenplays, you are writing what you love. What can else can you write? What else do you know better than what you love? When do you feel more on purpose, more at peace than when you are writing what you love, reading what you love, being with whom you love? Love is the language we all share. When I interview an author, I don't care that much about the book they've written. I care about how much they love the book. That's the interesting part to me because that's what we always have in common.

I understand now that writing used to be such an up-and-down experience for me because I didn't fully trust that all people are ultimately guided by love. I couldn't accept that love was, in fact, the very organizing force behind every life, bending our choices toward it as a flower grows toward the sun. Love, after all, is such an end in itself, wanting nothing more than itself, content with itself, at peace with itself. The world, meanwhile, was filled with violence and discontentment, filled with wanting and striving, with loss and gain. I had known all that myself, had known the wanting and the discontentment and the violence. And yet to sink into a story I was dreaming was to leave that world behind. Even though the stories I told were about that world and all its suffering, the telling occurred in a place where suffering was a stranger. Which was real? The dream of love or the world of pain? The choice was and still is mine to make, a choice I make with every story I write and every person I meet. I can find my connection to people where I find my connection to my stories if I remember to look for it no further than my own heart.

CHAPTER SEVEN

Full Engagement

One day I accompanied my son Jack and his second-grade class on their weekly trip to the local community center for swimming lessons. I was there theoretically to oversee the boys' locker room, but in reality I was there for Jack, to keep him focused on the job at hand. In those days, Jack spent far more time in his imaginary world than in the one he shared with other people. Some days, it seemed like he hardly visited our world at all.

My first job was simply helping him walk to the pool. The class lined up outside the school, a handful of adults in front and behind like shepherds, and we started out. While the other kids talked to one another or trundled along quietly, Jack began mumbling a story to himself, growling now and again and making claws of his fists. I hadn't been to his class in a while. It was one thing to see him pretending like this at home, it was another thing to see it in such stark contrast to the other kids.

Whatever story he was telling himself lasted the entire walk to the community center. It continued as all the kids plopped down in the waiting area outside the pool and began taking off their shoes and coats so they could go get changed. "Jack," I said. "Time to get your shoes and coat off."

He kept talking to himself, kept growling and making his claws. One by one the other kids got up and went into the locker room. Soon it was just the two of us, him with his coat and shoes on, and me losing my patience.

"Come on, Jack. You know what it's time to do."

He kept pretending.

"Shoes and coat, buddy."

He growled and made fists.

"Jack!" I grabbed his wrists. "Do you even want to be here?"

His eyes snapped into focus and he stopped pretending.

"Do you even want to be here?" I repeated.

He nodded and, like that, took off his shoes and coat and headed in to get changed.

I sat for a moment and took a breath. I wasn't sure if by "here" I meant school or life itself. It was a question I asked myself from time to time. I got up and followed Jack into the locker room, where, to my mild astonishment, he was changing into his swim trunks without my having told him to. This was one of the most confusing parts of being Jack's father when he was as boy. One moment he wouldn't respond to his name, the next he was talking to you about his day. It would have been simpler in a way if he never came out of his imaginary world. As it was, I never fully understood the rules of Jack's attention, what sent it inward and what drew it out.

The answer, I eventually came to understand, was exactly the same for Jack as everyone else. We raised Jack at a time when the concept of an autism *spectrum* first began to take hold. That is, there are children who exist on a broad spectrum of autistic behavior, from the kids who don't talk or take care of themselves, to children like Jack, and everything in between. The idea of the spectrum acknowledged that these kids were, in fact, all a little different, that you couldn't just lump them all into one tidy category. It was an important distinction, I felt, as it was a step toward treating these children with "special needs" more like everyone else. I never liked the term *special needs*, as it suggested my son were somehow made of different stuff than I was, as if kids labeled autistic were aliens. I had to see him as fundamentally like me, no matter how odd his behavior, and one of the quickest ways to do so was to admit that while I didn't flap and hum, I certainly retreated into an inner world when the one I was living in didn't please me. I had to accept that I, and probably everyone, was on the same spectrum as Jack.

Writers are particularly prone to this kind of retreat, I think. After it dawned on me that Jack's "pretending" was really just him making up stories, I'd ask him to share those stories with me. "No!" he'd protest. "They're private." How like a writer he was. Every writer wants, in theory, to share his or her work, to publish and get paid and experience the unique magic of seeing something we created in the sovereignty of our imagination inspire or entertain or inform a perfect stranger. But a great many writers worry that what seems so lovely and interesting and valuable in their imagination will be seen as dull and flat and valueless when exposed to the unforgiving attention of those same perfect strangers. Our stories, like children, are safe in our minds; the world of public opinion can seem far less safe. Anything can happen to a story when someone else reads it. It can be loved or ridiculed, embraced or rejected.

Likewise, the writer's journey *itself* can seem perilously uncertain. Many of my clients are adults who have full careers, careers they may have trained for in college, careers that send them every day to offices with coworkers or to classrooms with students. These are careers for which they are paid a known salary, hourly wage, or commission. When I was a waiter, every shift was a little different. Sometimes I had troublesome customers, and sometimes those customers and I got along like old friends. Sometimes I made $70, and sometimes I made $250; sometimes I had to stay to one o'clock in the morning, and sometimes I was home by nine PM. But I always knew that as long as that restaurant was open, I'd be there and leave with some cash in my pocket. And if it closed one day, I knew I could find another job somewhere else because the world always seems to need waiters.

None of this same certainty seems to apply to writing. Will the book I'm writing be published? What about the next one? Will I make any money off it? When I face a blank page in the morning, I don't really know what will fill it—if anything—by the end of my workday. It's tempting, as you begin your writing journey, to look at the path ahead and see it strewn with snares of rejection and the endless instability of the unknown. You may look at the path and wonder, "Is this just a *fantasy*? My job is real, but is this writing thing just some unreal dream?" You may wonder if your time at the desk is a bit like my son Jack's retreat into his imagination, an escape from what you know is reality, a reality that will wait for you until you stop pretending you're something you're not.

The last year I spent in the restaurant, something interesting started happening. Though I was still writing fiction, I had begun to think more and more about the relationship between creativity and spirituality, about free will and evolution. I was curious about where ideas came *from*, about my role in receiving these ideas, and about the relationship between what I thought and how I felt. There was a lot in my life about which I was uncertain, but one thing absolutely never changed: I *always* wanted to feel good. I assume that this is true for everyone. If something is true for everyone, it must be important. Maybe it is more important than anything else.

One of my best friends at work was another waiter named Tim. Tim was a very bright guy who, like a lot of waiters, had lived a pretty hard life. His had been filled with drug use, an abusive father, and even a brief stint in jail. But he'd recently begun to clean things up. He'd quit doing drugs, he was married, his first child was on the way, and he'd even begun an online business that was starting to take off. Tim liked to talk to me about the business, and I found myself offering him some counsel—not on business practices but on pursuing something for which there was no guaranteed outcome. Starting a business, like writing a book, requires a certain amount of trust. He'd come to me sometimes when he was feeling a little wobbly and I'd do my best to reassure him that he was going to be fine, that he didn't have to know exactly where the business was going, that he just needed to know that he wanted to create it.

To my surprise, I liked counseling Tim. It was like writing in a way, how when you tell a story you have to first go to that place within yourself where the stories exist. If you like to write, you know and like that place. The same is true of counseling someone. If you're going to tell someone that everything's going to be fine, which is mostly all you do, you have to first go to that place in yourself where you know everything's going to be okay. It's pretty much the same place I go to tell stories, except instead of inventing I'm just remembering.

As my time at the restaurant came to a close, I noticed myself offering this sort of counsel, support, and encouragement to other people in the restaurant. I say "noticed" because as I was doing it, and as I was understanding that I liked doing it, I sensed that I could have always been doing it if I had let myself. For years I had believed that that job provided only so many types of opportunities, that the pallet was necessarily limited and that I'd exhausted it. Yet here was another opportunity that I'd found only because I'd found it first in myself, the counsel I was offering my coworkers being an extension of what I'd noticed about the relationship between what I thought and how I felt.

Not long after leaving the restaurant, I took a short jaunt

to Los Angeles. My brother, John, was going to be there on a business trip, so I thought I'd rendezvous with him as well my old friend Chris. Now that I was out of the restaurant, I was thinking more and more about creativity and ideas and the relationship between what we think and how we feel. During the trip I started talking to Chris and John about all this interesting stuff. They seemed interested in listening to it. It was nice to have people to talk *to* instead of just thinking or muttering to myself. It was nice to clarify something when they seemed not to understand, and it was nice to recognize that what interested me interested other people as well, even if those other people were only my brother and my good friend.

Toward the end of the trip, Chris was driving me back to his house. As we wound through Los Angeles, I started talking again about creativity and spirituality, and Chris listened with interest. When I paused at the end of one thought, Chris said, "Bill, you know what you should be? You should be one of those guys I see on PBS sometimes pacing around on a stage talking about life and God and the meaning of it all. You should be one of those guys."

"You know what? I think you're right. I wonder how I'd do that?"

This was a good question. At that moment I was a more or less unpublished novelist who'd spent the last twenty years waiting tables. Who besides my friends would want to hear from me? Yet, strangely, there was nothing unreal to me about *this* new dream. There was only the question of how it would come to be. To be clear, I had no idea whatsoever *how* it would come to be; I had no point of reference, no first step even. All I *knew* was that it would be something I would enjoy doing, that I would like talking to groups of strangers about these ideas as much as I liked counseling Tim and talking to my friends and family about why it's so important that we all want to feel good all the time.

It turns out knowing I would enjoy doing something was and always is the first step. Which is to say, sitting in that car with Chris, I was already on my way toward making that dream, that idea, that life I could see only in my imagination. It was a reality—something I could see outside of my imagination. Not only had I taken the first step, I had taken the most *important* step, the one from which all other steps necessarily follow.

How do you write a book? First, you find an idea you're interested in. Without that, you have nothing. Without that character that speaks to you, without that "What if?", without the idea that wakes you up at night, you have no seed to plant from which the story grows. For me that idea was the relationship between creativity and happiness, that these two things were inexorably linked for everyone, whether they were writers or plumbers. Private ruminations became conversations with friends, conversations with friends became a personal blog, a personal blog became a magazine for writers, a magazine for writers became interviews with authors, interviews with authors became a podcast and more blogs and books. Every successful experience I've had were branches on a tree that sprouted from that single seed.

Jack is a young man now, and while he very much wants to go out into the world and get a job and have his own apartment and a girlfriend, he remains somewhat hampered by his habit of retreating into himself from that same world he wishes to explore. As his father, the best I can do now is to remind him that everything he wants in his outer life begins where he goes when he retreats. Every job, every relationship, every story we will tell begins within us, in a realm only we can possibly perceive. The only difference between retreating from life and full engagement with life is understanding that our imaginations are not a refuge from an unfriendly world, but the source for creating the world in which we would most like to live.

> *Every story we will tell begins within us.*

As I said, this is particularly important for writers. If you are a writer, you learned long ago that you are comfortable in your imagination. If you're a writer, you understood on some unspoken level that your relationship with what is normally called reality was slightly different than that of engineers or athletes or lawyers. Whether you had language for it or not, you knew that your inner world, the world only you could see, mattered as much to you as the outer world, the one everyone can see. We writers are not really any different from anyone else in this regard; we just usually spot this relationship sooner—though we often don't know what to do about it. We might even worry that there is something wrong with us, that we are too much in our heads, that we are too detached from reality.

But consider again my drive through Los Angeles with

Chris. When he told me he thought I might be the sort of person who talked about life and God and the meaning of it all, it was *real* that I had been waiting tables for the last twenty years, and it was *real* that I was a, more or less, unpublished novelist, and it was *real* that absolutely no one had ever asked me to talk to a group of any size about *anything*. But it was also real that I enjoyed talking to friends and family about these things, and that I always enjoyed thinking about these things, and that I would like to write about them once I could figure out a format to do so. All of that was real, too; it was just as real as all the other stuff. The question was, Which part of reality should I pay attention to? The first part wouldn't help me at all; there was nothing about it that could show me the way forward. Only my enthusiasm and desire could do that, so that's what I paid attention to.

By doing so, I wasn't ignoring *all* of reality, I wasn't putting my head in the sand. I was simply noticing the parts of reality I wanted more of. However, the moment I doubted the value of what I wanted to explore and share, which I did from time to time along this journey, I felt lost; in an instant, *nothing* seemed real. Doubting the value of what I value detaches me from my closest and most intimate connection to life itself. When I doubt what I value I am actually doubting my own value, doubting whether I have what it takes, whether I am good enough, whether I am worthy. I will never be able to prove my value; I will only know it as I know my own desires.

So go into your imagination. Dwell there. Daydream and drift away when it appeals to you. But be clear about what you're doing. Don't tell yourself you are escaping anything.

Don't pretend you're avoiding or ignoring. Accept that you are facing the source of all reality, that every book and building and business flowed from the same mysterious place. Everything great and terrible in the world began with a thought. You will never escape thinking, but you will always be able to choose what you think about, and in so doing choose the book, the life, the world you wish to create.

CHAPTER EIGHT

Failures

My father graduated from Harvard Divinity School, but by the time I arrived on the scene it had become clear to him that he was not put on this Earth to preach to the faithful. After my parents divorced, when I was seven, he spent several years searching: for work, for a place to live, for a relationship. He traveled to Greece alone for several months, got remarried, moved to Florida, then got divorced and moved back to Providence to be near his children again.

He tried to be a salesman. He tried selling something called a CheckWriter, which was supposed to prevent check fraud; he tried selling solar panels; he tried selling potting soil. He even tried selling Encyclopædia Britannica door-to-door. I accompanied him on one such outing. I had just turned eleven, and I followed him as he wandered through neighborhoods with chain-link fences and broken-down cars and barking dogs; accompanied him as he talked about the value of learning from expensive books to women staring back suspiciously from behind screen doors. He handled having doors slammed in his face pretty well.

The spring I turned thirteen he was unemployed, on food stamps, his car was about to be repossessed, and for the last two years he had moved from apartment to apartment, each one progressively smaller and in worse and worse neighborhoods, until he arrived on Bergen Street. He was being given a deal on a third-floor one-bedroom on a dead-end street because the landlord liked and took pity on him. I went with him the day he saw that apartment for the first time, following him up the dark, narrow staircase to the living room and kitchen area. The place was empty and had just been painted, but it still didn't feel clean. The ceiling sloped and the floorboards were stained.

My father looked around, poked his head into the bedroom. He was a man who had been raised in an upper middleclass family in Kansas City. His father had sold advertising for the *Kansas City Star,* and his mother had written *The Cub Scout Fun Book,* which I could still find at Sears and Roebuck. He'd been an Eagle Scout and a Unitarian minister. My father stood in the middle of this crappy apartment, on a street with no grass, no trees, where crushed tin cans and old newspapers and broken broom handles collected in the corners of empty parking lots, and nodded stoically. "Let's go," he said.

We got in his car, he reached for his keys but laid his hand on the wheel instead and sat for a moment, staring ahead at the road. My father was a man who always had a new idea cooking, but I sensed he was out of ideas at that moment. I didn't understand until then that to spend time with my dad was to also spend time with his ideas.

"If it's okay," he said, "I'm going to cry now."

And he did. I had noticed him crying once when we were watching a special on Judy Garland and once in a movie theater at the end of *Camelot*, but I had never seen him cry like this. Something collapsed in him: All at once, his face was streaked with tears, his lips quivering, the gulping sounds, his trembling hands on the steering wheel. We were so close to each other in the car with the windows up. I turned away, but I'd already seen him, and the sound of his weeping filled the car.

Soon enough the weeping stopped. I heard him sniff, and the car started. I glanced at him and he was wiping his face with his sleeve. "Thank you," he said.

"You're welcome."

We headed home. I was embarrassed for him and I was embarrassed for me. I hadn't wanted to see that, and not because I thought men or my father or anyone shouldn't cry, but because I feared that the potential for that collapse existed in everyone all the time. I was trying to figure out how to feel confident and competent in the world. I wanted to believe it was possible to cross some threshold where the fear and vulnerability of childhood was left behind once and for all. Seeing my father weeping reminded me that believing in such a threshold was like believing in Superman.

We were halfway home when my father started talking about Dungeons & Dragons. He had bought a copy of the game and he'd been playing it with my brother and sister and me. It was different from all the other games my family played because there were no winners and losers. The point of the game was to have fun. As we drove home, my dad started wondering what it was like to play with the people who'd actually invented the game, the *professionals*, if their adventures were more exciting than ours. I said I'd love to just sit in on one of their games, that I was sure there was something really cool they were doing that we just hadn't thought to do ourselves yet.

We talked about D&D all the rest of the way home. I knew we were decidedly *not* talking about what had happened. What had happened was like a silent passenger in the back seat we were choosing not to address. It was strange just ignoring that passenger, but at the same time, it was fun to talk to my dad in this way about the game. In fact, it would be the only time he and I would talk about it like this. It became a passion of mine just about the time he grew tired of it.

We never did talk about what had happened in the car that day—at least not directly. In some ways, though, he and I would always talk about it. Failure was a passenger in every drive we ever took. In fact, failure was a passenger of mine whether my dad was with me or not. I have been tempted over the years to lay my fear of failure at my father's doorstep, that watching him go broke and flounder for so many years cast a shadow over my own ambitions, but this would deprive me of the very gift that car ride home was meant to offer.

I THINK THE sight of failure is often worse than the experience of failure itself. I say this as someone who spent a good part of his adult life dreading he would fall off some professional cliff into an endless abyss. Once I dropped off the edge of the world, I believed I would find myself in a joyless, empty hell from which there was no return. Since I began teaching writing, I have learned I am not alone in this. Whenever I ask my students to describe what they believe failure is—that is, *complete* failure, the end-of-writing failure, end-of-trying failure—the answer is always the same: Nothing. An absolute nothingness.

I have never actually experienced nothing; I have only feared it. The closest I have come is when I have followed an idea while writing, followed it through narrower and narrower paths until that path dissipated altogether and I could find neither a way forward nor my belief that a way forward existed. Gone for the moment is the source of all my momentum. It can be an awful feeling, a walking-dead feeling, a life-has-no-point feeling. It's the sort of feeling that scares a lot of people from their desk, even though they very much love how it feels to have an idea they're following. The feeling of not having an idea can seem worse than how good it feels to actually have an idea. I was never scared away from the desk, but the fear of not having an idea did make writing a bit like a game of Russian roulette because I never knew for sure how far an idea would take me, whether it would lead me to the end I was seeking or the end I feared.

Writing stopped seeming like a game of Russian roulette once I realized that when I reached a dead end, I should step away from the desk, do something else, and come back. When I come back things are different. Sometimes what's different is I see a new way forward and sometimes what's different is I understand that I'm done with this particular idea, that it was the sort of idea that was attractive at first but not so much once it revealed itself to me. In either case, there is always something else, another way forward or another idea. Always something, never nothing.

This may seem like a very mundane solution to a very existential problem, and it is. But it is a solution that only works if I believe more in my *actual* experience than in what I imagine I *might* experience. I must believe more in reality than in nightmares.

This brings us back to the sight of failure. You'll see it everywhere if you want to: the panhandler on the street corner, the drug addict, the writer with ten unsold novels, the gymnast who falls from the balance beam, the father weeping in his car beside his son. If you want to believe that you have what it takes, that everyone has what it takes, you must make peace with all these images and more.

Because if you want to be a writer, you can't put *other* writers in a special category. If you want to publish books, then you must believe that your book belongs on the same shelf with Stephen King or Tolstoy or Toni Morrison or Virginia Woolf. Your books will be on that same bookshelf, after all. And when someone wanders a bookstore, your book might be right next to King's or Morrison's, and that reader might choose yours. To the reader looking for the right book for *them*, there is no scale of worthiness; there is only preference. The shelf is as neutral as a blank page. Anyone can be there, including you.

You have to accept this. It may even feel a little disappointing. Maybe you hoped publishing a book would help you at last feel as special, as valuable, as worthy as you imagined you could. It won't. To accept that you belong on the shelf is to accept that the book is an expression of *what* you value, not evidence *of* your value. No matter how many books you publish, no matter how many awards you win, you will wake up tomorrow feeling more or less like you do now. You will still and always be you.

It's what you've always wanted, and why you can't fear the sight of what we call failures. When we fear the failure we see, when we take pity on it, we are putting it, or those people, in a special category. Just as I could not raise my son Jack if I saw him as uniquely special, as somehow different than I, somehow inherently less capable, so too I cannot see people suffering in their unhappiness, whose books didn't sell, whose marriage fell apart, whose business went broke, as somehow different than you or I. You can have compassion for these suffering people without taking pity on them, without telling yourself a tragic story about them. To have compassion for them is to see them like yourself; to have pity on them is to see them as different from you.

How are they like you? They have simply reached the end of an idea. Sometimes we are so committed to an idea, as I was when I thought I would be a novelist, that we do not allow any other ideas into our minds. So, we follow and follow that idea, whether it's a relationship or a business or a book; follow it like a dog on a scent, until there is no more scent. If we're lucky, another idea is waiting there to take its place. That's not usually how it goes. First, we have to grieve the end of that idea, of all that we hoped to gain from it, grieve the loss of momentum we felt following it. That momentum felt like the flow of life itself, the meaning of life, our purpose and place. Now it's gone. It's like a death in the family. How will we ever be happy again?

The grieving can be as short or as long as we want it to be. Once the grieving has ended, we are ready for a new idea. Of course, we have to believe there *are* new ideas, just as there are new lovers or new businesses. That is, stories, lovers, and businesses will be everywhere, but if we don't believe in them, we won't see them. Writing teaches me this every day. I simply cannot see the way forward in what I'm writing, cannot find the idea for the next essay, if I don't believe I have an idea or if I believe there is no way forward. If I sit at my desk thinking, *I've got nothing*, I'll have nothing. It's like closing the door to where ideas come from. But if I ask, "What have I got today?" I've opened that door. It doesn't mean something will come through right away, but eventually it will. It always does.

But something only comes if I open that door and leave it open. If I don't, if I close it with my disbelief, my doubt, I will find myself in the very nothing I have always feared. I'll wallow in deep, bitter darkness. When I've been in this state, I've wanted people to take pity on me. Poor Bill. My despair was what made me special. I'd seen the void. Oh, you people who still have hope, who still believe. How delightful must be your fantasies of a just world, a kind world, a fertile world. Your beliefs, like my ideas, will run their course and then you'll come join me.

I wasn't much fun to hang around with when I was like this. Fortunately, I could never stay too long in the wasteland.

As I said, ideas are always coming. Though it doesn't seem like it at the time, keeping the door to ideas closed takes some effort. It's willful, a kind of loyalty to the old idea that takes the shape of grief and despair. Eventually, I get distracted or exhausted or forget to keep a vigilant watch over my despair, and in this stillness, something comes. I could always reject that new idea, and sometimes I do. Usually, though, my loyalty to despair is not as strong as my desire to live, to create something new, to be happy.

This process of old and new ideas repeats itself again and again every time I write. Every time I delete a sentence I've written, I go through some tiny version of this. Having deleted so many sentences in my writing life, the transition from grief to acceptance is so fast I don't perceive it. I hardly notice, if at all, that tiny resistance, the thought, *But I wrote that!* Like an arborist pruning a tree, I know the sentence must go. As soon as it's gone, I'm relieved. It was cluttering things up, taking me somewhere I didn't want to go. I may have loved writing it, enjoyed finding each word. Why, I may have discovered something about writing in finding that sentence, might have even learned something about myself! Doesn't matter. That darling did indeed have to die to make room for what was needed in my story. The circle of life.

What we call failure is really just resistance. We are resisting what comes next. We are resisting our natural selves, our natural ability to receive new ideas and take new directions. Resistance is uncomfortable and depressing and hopeless. But it also takes effort. Most of the time, we drop our resistance eventually. Sometimes, however, we don't. There are people who hold on to their resistance right up until their death. This does not mean they were incapable of dropping that resistance, just that they didn't. I reject the notion anyone is incapable of dropping their resistance. If I am the one holding it, I can drop it. New ideas, new stories, new life will come.

It certainly did for my father. There was nothing wrong with us talking about Dungeons & Dragons during that car ride. That was a new idea. It cheered us up. Neither of us wanted to wallow in his grief. Yes, we were both straining a bit against the momentum of despair, but our attention was forward. About three months later, my dad told me he'd gotten interested in learning how to survive in his new circumstance, how he rode a bike now or took the bus, how he'd learned how to feed himself on a small budget. He enrolled in college classes and learned how to program computers. Three years later, he had remarried, had a job at a company downtown, and was living in a big house in a lovely neighborhood.

Then he got divorced again. And he went broke again. But then he got married again! And he got a new job again! But then he lost that job and got a new one. So it went. He's still married at eighty-five. He called my mom when she turned eighty to welcome her into that new decade. He told her his eighties were the happiest time of his life. He teaches English as a Second Language to Brown grad students in his house and plays complicated war games on his computer and has long conversations with his wife.

For good or bad, it is often easier to see yourself in your parents and your children than a stranger on the street or a celebrity on TV. A family is like a shared idea for how life should be led, what's important and what's trivial, what's possible and what's a dream. At some point, everyone in the family must follow that idea somewhere different, discovering that what was seen as trivial in the clan was actually important to them personally, or what was believed to be only a dream by the family was quite attainable with sustained attention. After everyone's left the nest, found their own homes, and started their own families, they sometimes gather together again. Sometimes this goes well and sometimes it doesn't. The tensions of all their different directions, their different ideas, sometimes turns holidays and birthday parties into one ongoing argument about how life should be led.

But sometimes the family is able to rest within what they still agree on, which is usually love, the source of all the good ideas anyone will ever have. It's why love does not recognize what we call failure. Love is forever growing and forever supporting, forever expanding and forever giving. We fall down, and in our wretched state feel like nothing, feel ashamed of our failure, feel ashamed of what we couldn't do. Love does not see a wretched creature, does not see something unworthy. It is waiting, as always, with the next thing, the next thought, the next idea, instantly and forever forgiving you for believing you were anything less than anyone else.

CHAPTER NINE

Earthly Powers

My uncle Loyd had been training to be a Navy pilot when he got polio and lost the use of both his legs. He married my mom's older sister, Sally, not long after leaving the Navy, and they moved to Kansas City. My mom was close to Sally, and we'd visit every other summer or so. I have no memory of the first time I met Loyd in the same way I have no memory of the first time I saw my mother's face. Like the seasons or school or television, Loyd in his wheelchair was a fact of life.

I did see a single picture of him before he had polio. I was twelve and discovered it while rummaging around Sally and Loyd's house one rainy afternoon. It was from his days in the Navy, and there was a young Loyd in a crew cut, smiling through the pilot's window of a fighter jet. Here was the face of a man who, like me, assumed he'd spend the rest of his life walking and running. It was all he'd ever known, it was reality—until it wasn't. It struck me that even in this picture he was sitting. I felt it was better for me that I had no image of him standing, as I was less tempted to feel sorry for him.

If Loyd felt sorry for himself, he never betrayed it to me. Sometimes he'd grouse when he was getting in and out his car and needed to fold up his wheelchair. If it didn't fold easily enough, he'd say, "This dern thing." The most upset I ever saw him when I was a child was when we were fishing and his favorite lure, a "carrot top," snapped free of his line when he was casting in the shallows. We spent the next twenty minutes searching for it, motoring back and forth through the weeds. He even had me climb out and check the shoreline of the little muddy island we'd been fishing near. I hoped I'd find it just so we could get back to fishing and having fun.

I was surprised he cared that much about the lure. He seemed like a man who knew how to let things go. I was unaware of the victories and disappointments of life sticking to him. It was a strength of perspective I vaguely associated with him being in a wheelchair—though not because he seemed to have accepted something someone else might not have accepted, but because sitting itself was such a grounding position. Sitting was how you relaxed and contemplated and regained your sense of balance. Sitting was what you did when you stopped trying so hard to *get somewhere*. Sitting said you had nowhere to be at the moment. Loyd was always sitting.

I never thought of Loyd as *handicapped*. I understood the word technically applied to him, though it did not align with my experience of my uncle. Loyd got from one place to another using a wheelchair; I got from one place to another walking. We were different in that way, but I was different from everyone in some way. For instance, when I was a boy, I was always the fastest one of my friends. For a time, it was part of my identity, this thing I knew how to do. It never occurred to me not to talk about running around Loyd, though I rarely did. I wasn't worried that it would be insensitive, but being near him I was reminded of the value of stillness, and it made me want to find that same stillness in myself.

WHEN I WAS twenty, I picked up my first copy of James Joyce's *Ulysses*. I'd heard a lot about the book and decided it was time to see what the fuss was all about. I admit I was as much intrigued by the concept of *Ulysses* as anything else: that it was brilliantly experimental, that it was unlike any other book, and that it was largely considered the Greatest English-Language Novel Ever Written. When I got home with my new copy, I felt like I was about to open a sacred text, that reading it would take me somewhere I'd never imagined traveling before.

That wasn't quite my experience, though I did love how Joyce could find the poetry and meaning in the smallest of moments. This seemed like no small feat to me from a technical standpoint, but also from a spiritual one. If you aren't familiar, *Ulysses* takes place in one day (June 16, 1904, to be exact) in Dublin, and follows the crisscrossing paths of Leopold Bloom and Stephen Dedalus. The novel's "plot" mirrors that of Homer's *Odyssey*, though not a lot actually *happens* in a dramatic sense. Mostly, the two men walk around and talk to people and think about stuff.

This is exactly what I found so compelling about it. Mostly, all I did was walk around and think about stuff, and talk to people about what I'd been thinking, and think about what I'd just talked about. All this walking and thinking and talking could seem kind of meaningless, an endless hamster wheel of words and ideas. Reading *Ulysses* reminded me that if I was honest, I didn't believe all my talking and thinking was meaningless. Life was meaningful, and since I was alive, my thinking and talking must be meaningful. That's what I took from that book, anyway. Whether that's what Joyce wanted me to take away from it, I don't know. I never met the man.

Also, from a pure writing standpoint, I appreciated the care with which he rendered the physical world. I thought Joyce was very painterly in his depiction of things. There seemed to be no drive in him to move, move, move the story forward. I thought of this when I read Stephen Dedalus's definition of "proper art" in A *Portrait of the Artist as a Young Man*. Dedalus says art should be characterized by stasis, not movement, that the artist should "behold" the world, not crave it or fear it.

I agreed with that, though largely because that stillness I perceived in my uncle often eluded me. I'd read and enjoyed plenty of books that cracked along at a happy pace. And I couldn't actually finish *Ulysses*, though I tried several times. I got lost in some of his experiments and didn't have the curiosity to unpack what he was up to. But I stayed interested in the book as a kind of beacon of Great Literature. So many books were written, and yet it seemed to stand alone in a way none other did. I liked that it could do that for a number of reasons, none of which, however, had much to do with the world being made of creative equals.

Not long after I moved in with my wife, and about the time I'd started my first novel, I stumbled onto a PBS documentary about *Ulysses*. I settled right in. The documentary included dramatized scenes from the novel and from Joyce's life (including one where the author is shown relaxing in his flat after a hard day of writing, explaining to a friend that he's trying to finish a single sentence, that he has all the words but just hadn't found their correct order yet), as well as interviews with authors and academics about the novel's significance and meaning.

One of those authors was the British novelist Anthony Burgess. Like a lot of artsy young men of my age, I first became aware of Burgess when I saw Stanley Kubrick's adaptation of his novel *A Clockwork Orange*. After seeing the movie, I tried reading the book, but I couldn't get into it. I also tried one of his other dystopian novels but couldn't get into that, either. I didn't know it at the time, but I was in the process of discovering a lifelong dislike for dystopian fiction. I was a closet optimist in those days.

However, for Christmas my senior year in high school, I got a paperback version of Burgess's massive, sweeping, twentieth-century epic *Earthly Powers*. It seemed like the first really grown-up book I'd read. The narrator is a gay novelist, his brother-in-law is a famous Catholic bishop, and the book is filled with famous writers and historical references, all mixed together in a compelling saga of a story. I loved it, devouring the book at home and at school. The young writer in me also noticed some things Burgess did stylistically, how he often left out certain details that I would have included, and how leaving those things out actually brought the scenes more fully to life in my imagination.

So when Burgess appeared in the documentary, I felt like I was getting a twofer. Though it had been almost ten years, I still remembered reading *Earthly Powers*, still felt a debt of gratitude toward what it had opened up to me. Burgess, it turns out, was a Joycean expert of sorts, having written a study of the Irish novelist's work. He spoke lovingly of *Ulysses's* influence on the modern novel and on his own work, of Joyce's acrobatic facility with language, and of all the tricky, secret referential morsels scattered throughout the story, how a person could spend a lifetime deciphering its elaborate code.

He concluded his summation with a devotional sigh. "You know," he said, "it's quite simply the greatest English-language novel ever written. Period. The rest of us just have to accept that and carry on as best we can."

I stopped liking the documentary right then. I hated hearing Burgess rank himself in this way, even if it was in comparison to Joyce. *Earthly Powers* had meant as much to me as *Ulysses*, maybe more. It was different, but just as necessary. Plus, I wasn't sure if I believed him. I heard something disingenuous in his genuflecting at Joyce's feet that I recognized in myself. I would later learn that Burgess described himself as a "monarchist with a distaste for all republics." It struck me that he and I were both trying to make a king of Joyce and his enigmatic book. If you believe in kings, and you don't think you're one, you'll need to figure out who is.

Here's an interesting fact about crowns: Typically, they are smooth and flat at the bottom where they rest on the monarch's head but are pointed on top. Those points are meant to represent the direct connection between the royal and God. They're like antennae. I fully understand the desire to be led by someone who is himself in constant and unfiltered communication with someone or something that is all knowing and all loving, who is guided by love at all times, unburdened by the crippling needs of the insatiable ego. To such a person, every step of the way forward would be lit brightly, and they need only walk it, and we—we whose legs and backs are bent from the weight of fear and indecision and ceaseless wanting— need only to follow.

I have crowned more than a few artists in my life. Where their work had taken me felt like a kind of heaven, a place free of the daily, grinding, nameless suffering I often endured. How miraculous a single story or poem or song can seem when it lifts that suffering, even when that story or song or poem tells of sadness and heartbreak, how it seems to purge you of the heartache and sadness you carry. What a relief.

At their peak, when Beatlemania was literally sweeping the globe, parents with children who couldn't walk or talk, who were deaf or blind, would find their way to the band's dressing room after shows and plead to have their children touched by one of the Fab Four. They believed their children would be healed. The Beatles, after all, had displaced Elvis Presley as the kings of rock and roll.

The problem with kings in reality—and by "reality" I mean that to which I actually awaken every morning—is that the concept of royalty assigns all creative power to someone else. Every day I awaken to a countless string of choices I must make, from the clothes I'll wear, to the breakfast I'll eat, to the words I'll speak. These are all choices I have to make. Why, it's like a story itself, isn't it? That blank page will not fill itself. Every word I put there is a choice. No king can choose those stories or scenes or words for me. Like it or not, I must make those choices alone, within the absolute sovereignty of my singular imagination.

Though on a good day, which is most days now, I feel as though I'm making those choices in collaboration with something or someone else. I used to think I was doing it alone. I was by myself, after all. But as a writer I value accuracy, and it would be inaccurate to describe writing as anything other than a relationship. I ask a question and then receive an answer. That's how it works. It makes writing much easier. I don't have to know everything. I only have to know what I'm interested in, what questions I want to ask. If I know the question I want to ask, the answer always comes. The answer won't come, however, if I think some questions are worth asking and some are not or that some stories are worth writing and some are not. Or, for that matter, that some lives are worth living and some are not.

One afternoon Jack and I had gone to a local mall to buy him a book and have some ice cream. We were sitting in the food court when I noticed a man in a wheelchair being pushed about by a caregiver. This was not a wheelchair like my uncle's. This was an electric wheelchair for quadriplegics, complete with a keyboard for typing out basic messages. The man's head drooped to one side, his mouth hung open slightly, and his hand gestured erratically.

I felt a surge of pity and fear. I thought how glad I was that I was neither of these men. I was glad I didn't have to care for someone with these kinds of needs. How all-consuming. How would I ever write a story? All my attention would be on him. And I thought how glad I was that I wasn't the man in wheelchair, that I had the use of all my limbs, and that I could speak and run and jump and make love.

It made me sad to think this way. So I looked away, looked at the crowded food court, at everyone eating their lunch or drinking their coffee and having their conversations. It occurred to me then that I didn't want to be any of *those* people, either, all of whom could walk and talk and jump and run. I didn't want to be them, and I didn't want to be James Joyce or Anthony Burgess or Paul McCartney. I wanted to be me. I wanted to be me even though I hadn't sold as many books as I thought I should, even though some days I woke up and wondered what the point of it all was, even though I worried and doubted, even though my back and knees and shoulder hurt sometimes, even though I lost my temper, even though I got bored and frustrated. I still didn't want to be anybody else. I didn't want to be anyone else, and I didn't want to write anyone else's stories.

And so why shouldn't this be true of that man in the wheelchair also? Why shouldn't he want to be him and live *his* life even though there were things he surely wished were different about it? Either every moment and every circumstance and every life has meaning, or no moment and no circumstance and no life has meaning. There is no in between.

I've noticed with some sympathy the challenge people have in public conversations describing paraplegics or quadriplegics or children on the autism spectrum. When I was a boy, the terms *disabled* and *retarded* were used pretty casually. Those days are gone, the epithets replaced with the clunky *differently abled* or *nonneurotypical*. I don't chalk this linguistic transition up to mere political correctness. *Disabled* and *retarded* were not just unkind, but also inaccurate.

What they should be replaced with, I don't really know. The truth is, not everyone's able to do the exact same things, just as not everyone's able to write the same kinds of stories. But everyone is *able* to hear what speaks to writers when they write, that universal guidance that answers those questions we ask, whether we are asking about the stories we tell or the homes we buy or lovers we choose. It speaks to me as it spoke to Joyce as it speaks to you. And every story you tell will grow in some way from the unique circumstances of your unique life, the unique challenges and limitations, the unique pain you carried and released, the unique victories and disappointments. Your life has never happened before and will never happen again. You alone are tasked with telling the stories that grow from it.

Meanwhile, as you go about the world, know that your life and your stories are also a source of inspiration to all the other storytellers out there. Mostly, like my uncle, and Joyce, and Burgess, and that man in the wheelchair, you'll never know

how you inspired someone else. Perhaps, however, you'll publish something and a grateful reader will contact you. They
will try to put into words what your story meant to them, how
what you shared changed them in some small way. You'll
thank them for their generosity, but without fully understanding what was given and what was received. Their unique life
remains slightly mysterious to you. No matter. In their gratitude you'll be reminded that whether we write stories or care
for the infirm or march in the streets, we are all here for one
another, everyone teaching everyone the value of their life.

CHAPTER TEN

Getting in the Mood

I've been writing six days a week for nearly thirty years. I've always written first thing in the morning, arriving at my desk with trainlike punctuality. I never skip a day, and I always produce something. Often, it goes pretty well. I get in The Flow and lose track of time and my stories end up taking surprising and satisfying turns. If it starts going *really* well, I have to jump out of my chair and pace around my workroom muttering to myself. The ideas are so interesting to me I can't wait to tell other people about them, even if those other people are imaginary. By the end I feel both calm and motivated, eager to do something else but content if I can't think of what that something else will be.

If it sounds pretty good to you, that's because it is. Yet as nice as it is, as inspiring and life-affirming as it is, I am never in the mood to write when I sit down to begin. Never. I'm usually stone cold.

In fact, because I write a lot of essays or books like this that are essentially comprised of a bunch of long essays, I often begin without the luxury of being able to read what I wrote the day before. Often, I'm staring at a blank page wondering what the hell I'm going to write about today, sometimes feeling as if I've said absolutely all there is to say about those things that interest me most. It's not a great feeling. It's the sort of feeling that, if I didn't encounter it as often as I did, might lead me to believe I wasn't cut out for this writing thing. Writers, after all, like to write. Writers have ideas. Most mornings I start by thinking, *I've got nothing.*

It took me many years to understand why it often begins this way for me and for many other people as well. In fact, the more I came to understand about this first moment, this sitting in the same chair every morning and feeling like writing happens somewhere miles away from me, the more I understood that this moment of temporary emptiness is what frightens so many beginning authors away from pursuing writing as deeply as they would like. After all, if everyone indeed has what it takes, if everyone has a natural curiosity and is naturally connected to the very source of all the inspiration and ideas they'll ever need, why then do we so often sit and feel like we have no ideas, no inspiration, no interest in this thing we were very interested in yesterday? If, as I sometimes complain, "I've got nothing," then I certainly don't *have* what it takes. You have to have *something* if you're going to have what it takes.

Part of the challenge has to do with the unique nature of writing. Unlike every other art form, writing does not employ any of the five senses. Writers try to simulate, reference, and describe the sights and sounds and smells and tastes of the world, but writing and reading are *entirely* imaginary. Musicians use their bodies to create a sound that another person can physically hear. Painters use their bodies to create images on a canvas that another person can physically see. So too with actors using their bodies and voices. Writers, meanwhile, traffic entirely in thought. A sentence is a thought. You can't touch it or hear it or smell it or taste it. Ultimately, the story is told where there is no sight or sound or touch or smell. I happen to love that place, am fascinated by it. You probably are, too. If you're a writer, then you're interested in rendering the three-dimensional, five-sensory, temporal world using nothing but thoughts.

All of which I mention because you are not just a writer, you are also a human, someone who gets about the world entirely dependent on those five senses. Not only do you use your eyes and ears and hands to navigate streets and shopping malls and conversations and recipes, those eyes and ears are also the connective portals to inspiration. That world I can see and hear is a constant source of new ideas. It begins as soon as I wake up. I open my eyes and there is my bedroom and my wife beside me. I can hear the birds outside my window. Do birds even sleep? I can't picture it. My wife sits up and gives me a hug and a kiss on the cheek. We'd been away from each other in our separate dreamlands, but now we're together again. I make coffee and the smell reminds me of when my grandmother visited from Missouri when I was eight, sitting with her in our kitchen before anyone else was awake as she ate her toast and drank her coffee. I feed the cat and she makes her happy chirping sounds as I fill her dish. I think how much I communicate with her without words, how I know what she wants by how she moves around my feet, how she looks at me. Unloading the dishwasher, I decide, is like putting yesterday away, each plate and glass and fork the last remains of our meals; as soon as they're back in their cabinets and drawers, those dishes belong to today. I go to my desk and I can see the new e-mails that have arrived, can see who sent them and can guess what they're about. Tricky to read them now. It's like starting a conversation with someone. Better to jump into writing. I open a file. I look at the page. Nothing.

Why nothing? Well, first of all, I'm looking at a blank page. It gives me nothing. In the fifteen minutes it took me to go from my bed to the desk I had already seen and heard much that stimulated ideas and memories. I didn't really have to *do* anything to receive that stimulation. Simply existing in the physical world with my five senses provided me with plenty of ideas. It seemed to just happen. Now, facing this blank page, I can no longer depend on *that* world for new thoughts. To write, I have to go within for all my stimulation and inspiration. I have to go where my five senses are of no use, are, in fact, a distraction.

This can take time. It doesn't have to take a *lot* of time, but it will take time. It's like I've been in a conversation with the world—with my wife and the birds and the cat and the coffee and the dishes—but now I want to have a new conversation. I can't think about the coffee and my grandmother if I want to write about my father and his crappy apartment on Bergen

Street. A conversation has its own momentum, a momentum that starts as soon as that conversation begins. I have to let the momentum of that old conversation slow to a stop before I can find the new one. I can't have two conversations at once.

I became a more prolific and confident writer when I started taking this shift from external focus to internal focus seriously, when I began recognizing that I had to do something with my attention before I could write, that I had to allow myself to get *into* the mood to write. It was an important realization because it meant I could stop fretting about the experience of feeling as though I had nothing to write about. Or, I should say, the realization allowed me to fret considerably less.

To take this shift seriously, I can't be intimidated by the blank page. It's a terrible, empty feeling to believe you have nothing, have no ideas, have no interest in writing. For me, thinking that I have no interest in writing—which I still sometimes do—is like thinking I having no interest in living. This threat of nothingness can make sitting down to write seem perilous, a looming encounter with your creative mortality. It's a false threat. All that's happening when I'm looking at the blank page is that I am still feeling the momentum—the creative momentum, mind you—of my domestic life, am still feeling that conversation, the heat and interest of those ideas, while trying to start a new conversation with my writing mind.

This is why the first thing I must do to get into the mood to write is to forget. I have to let myself forget about the life I lead outside my door. It doesn't matter that I actually write *about* the world, that I tell stories about what happened to me thirty years or three days ago; I'm not writing about the world I live in at that moment. I have to forget about my bills, forget about that e-mail from my agent, about what my sons are up to, about that thing my wife said last night; I have to forget about politics and sports and the news and the weather. I have to let it all go. It'll all be there when I'm done writing. But to get into the mood to write, I can't believe that any of that is more deserving of my attention than that blank page.

Once I've let that world go, my mind is still enough, is empty enough—indeed is *blank* enough—that I can begin to find that new conversation. It doesn't take much at all. Usually, one interesting sentence will do it. I may not know where that sentence is leading, how long the story it wants to tell will be or how it will end—I may not even know how the next sentence should begin. Doesn't matter. That single sentence is like the first embers of a fire. It has my attention, and my attention is like the breath from a bellows, spreading the heat to the next sentence and the next sentence and the next sentence, and now I'm in the mood, and now I'm writing.

Here is yet another reason we mustn't fear the blank page. The nothingness, the emptiness of the blank page is actually what allows us to get into the mood to write. We need that stillness, that clean slate, in order to find the new idea. The blank page says, "You can write *anything*. Nothing is begun. Nothing is in process. There is nothing to react to, nothing to avoid, nothing that requires your response. Absolutely anything can be here, and the page will remain perfectly blank until you make a choice."

I sometimes work with life coaches or public speakers who

would like to write a book. These are men and women who love to communicate, who are often comfortable in front of large groups of people. They have a message, and they love sharing it. And yet when they sit down to put this message onto the page, they feel disconnected and unmotivated. I thought it was a quirk the first time I encountered it, but I have heard this complaint from these clients again and again.

I understood their challenges better the more *I* coached. I'm a writing coach, but also a bit of a life coach, helping my clients learn how not just to write better, but also how to live as a writer, to be self-employed, to depend entirely on their internal creativity for their livelihood. In short, I coach what I write about. I love the coaching because the clients all come with their own unique challenges, their own unique questions. Sometimes two clients have the same sort of challenge, but what I told the first does not help the second. Now I have to think about the problem anew, to look at it differently. In this way, their troubles, their questions, have inspired me, have helped me better understand the very thing I am helping them understand.

Moreover, a client or a workshop full of students often provides instant energy. I arrive at a writers' conference to teach Fearless Writing. I've taught it many times, have told many of the same stories again and again. If it goes well, in the two or three hours I spend teaching that class I might find one or two new ways to explain old concepts. Mostly, however, I am a bit like a stand-up comedian who has learned his material. And yet as soon as the class starts, as soon as I look out at those faces of the writers who have not yet heard what I am about to say, whose attention is like a blank page waiting to be filled, it is easy to find my enthusiasm for this material again. Because it's new to them, it feels new to me. No, not new—just interesting. It's still interesting to me, it's still inspiring to me, still worthy of my attention, and if I allow myself to get into it fully, it feels as hot and clear as when I first found it. It's like love. I married someone many years ago, have memorized her face, we have told each other every story there is to tell, and yet it takes only a word, a look, a touch from her to feel again that first pinprick of love that caught my attention the way a new story arrives demanding to be told.

How strange and depressing then when a life coach or inspirational speaker sits down to write and cannot find that fresh, hot, clear interest in her material. It's like thinking you've fallen out of love with your spouse. Suddenly the road ahead looks barren. Everything good in the world grows from love and you've got none of it. Horrible. It's why one speaker I worked with told me, "I know I need a book, but I just hate writing. I hate it more than anything." I don't blame her. Who wants to feel, if only for a moment, as if the light that guides and warms has gone out for good?

It's not gone, of course. It's like the sun. It's there shining at midnight, though all you can see of it is its reflection on the moon. Except when I see the moon I never think of the sun. I look upon it as a dim lantern of the night, shining its own independent pale light, surrounded by its host of silver stars. How easy it is for my eyes to misunderstand the source of what lights the world.

This is why writing has been so helpful to me. Because

sometimes I wake up and though I hear the birds I don't receive their song. It's just another morning noise like the squeak of my box spring as I climb out of bed. Did my wife kiss me? Probably. I've already forgotten. Now the coffee's brewing and the cat needs to be fed and the dishwasher unloaded. It's just stuff that needs to be done, the endless cycle of domestic maintenance. The thoughts that come are old ones, as familiar as the chores themselves, as the kitchen and the mudroom and the furniture. Everything's familiar, everything's been done before and held before and seen before and heard before. I take my coffee to my desk and there it is, the same blank page. There it is, asking its same eternal question: *What do you want today?*

This is when the blank page is my friend. It reminds me where to find the light I've lost sight of. The world I roam around in, the birds and the coffee and my cat and even my wife's kisses, are like the moon, made bright only by the light of my interest in life itself. The world I see can only reflect that light, it cannot create it, cannot give it. I sit down to write not to light a fire but only to find the source of that illumination once more. Find it, and the way forward through a story is lit; find it, and the fuel of enthusiasm burns, carrying me on without effort; find it, and I am alive again, reminded that no moment can ever be the same as the last.

CHAPTER ELEVEN

Why Publish?

I f you had asked me why I waited tables, I would have said, "For the money." This was true in its own way. It was how I fed my family and paid my mortgage. And I wouldn't have waited one table if I hadn't been paid to do so. But when I thought about the actual *experience* of working in restaurants, it was never the money that came to mind. Sometimes it was the stress and disappointment, but mostly it was the people, my coworkers and the customers. They were the interesting and enlivening part, the reason I learned and laughed. I also liked the performative nature of being a waiter, and the mental challenge of serving five or six tables simultaneously. I only thought about the money when I wasn't working, and then mostly to wish I had more of it.

While I was waiting those tables and writing novels, I thought often about wanting to have my work published. I did not, however, ever think about *why* I wanted to publish my stories. It seemed like an absurd question. I was a writer. Writers publish their stuff. You publish your stuff because there's no other way to make a living as a writer. Moreover, I was sure that publishing a book would answer all kinds of nagging questions about myself, chief among them, of course, was whether I had what it took. So, I never thought about why I wanted to publish; it would have been like asking why I wanted to eat and breathe.

However, one day my wife learned about an interesting kinesthetic test you could take to determine how truthful you're being with yourself. You hold your arm out straight at shoulder height, and someone asks you a question, gently pressing down on your arm as they do so. If you're being honest, you have the strength to keep your arm straight; if you're being dishonest, you lose that strength and the person can push your arm down.

It sounded like fun, so we gave it a try. I held my arm out and she asked me my name. "Bill Kenower," I answered, and my arm held firm. She asked again, and I said, "Filmore McSwain," and, sure enough, I lost all strength and down went the arm. It worked! We tried it with a few other questions— did I think I was a nice person (yes), did I like being a father (also yes)—and then she surprised me:

"Do you want to publish this novel?"

"Yes, I want to publish the novel."

All the strength drained out of my shoulder, and my arm collapsed.

"What the hell?" I said. "I *want* to publish it."

"Maybe you don't. That's interesting, isn't it?"

"It's bullshit, is what it is."

The problem was I didn't think it was bullshit, though I had no idea what to do with this information, and so I carried on as before. Years later, I decided to publish a collection of my essays from *Author*. My reasons for doing so were quite practical. I was starting to teach some workshops and do public speaking, and I thought if I had a book to sell—a "back of the room sale," as it's called—I could make a little extra money at these gigs. I thought at first I would self-publish, and went about choosing which essays I wanted to include, selecting a font, and learning how to lay out a book.

There was one moment in the middle of this process, as I was putting the essays in order, that I thought—no, *realized*—that I absolutely loved this little book. *I would buy this book*, I thought, *if I weren't publishing it*. It was the first book I had written that I'd not burdened with any real requirements beyond simply existing. I didn't need it to prove I was talented, or smart, or important, or worthy. I just wanted it to be in the world.

I ended up publishing the book with a very small publisher, though since I'd done so much work on it already, this felt more like a business arrangement than *actually* publishing a book. Still, it was nice to have the help, and I liked the cover design they came up with, and I was happy when my box of complimentary copies arrived.

Then I wrote *Fearless Writing*. Or, I should say, I met a woman who thought she could sell a book based on the classes I had been teaching. I told her I didn't want to write a book for writers, I wanted to write a book for *everyone*. She said it would be much, much easier to sell if I made it for writers, so I said, "Fine. Writers it is."

I wrote some sample chapters and a proposal. I was glad she had talked me into targeting writers. It focused the book in a way I would not have anticipated. This was the first time I had worked with someone else in this fashion on a book, had been willing to take their guidance. I was surprised that my normal creative stubbornness did not object. I got some endorsements from writers I knew and we sent it off to a half dozen publishers.

I noticed something was different in me. I'd had several agents before, and they'd all sent my work off to publishers, but the idea of someone actually buying my books seemed unreal to me. I was always disappointed when the manuscripts didn't sell, but a part of me never expected them to. In fact, if I'd allowed myself to be perfectly honest, it was as if they were not supposed to sell. That feeling of one part of me wanting something and the other not was absolutely confounding.

For this book, however, I didn't notice that split in me. At least not at first. A couple weeks after the proposals went out, we got our first rejection. This was on a Friday. Reading the agent's e-mail, I felt an old familiar disappointment, felt exactly as I had with all the other books that had gone out and been rejected. On that Friday, however, I remembered the time my wife tested my arm strength. So, I asked myself the question: *Do you want to publish this?*

The first honest answer I got was, *No.*

Specifically, I didn't *want* to publish it, I *needed* to publish it. I needed to publish it to prove I'd finally won the writing game, finally proved I was good enough, that I had what it took. It was as if I'd created a disapproving parent in my mind who wouldn't love me until I'd proved I was worthy of being loved. I'd show him, though. I'd just keep failing until he loved me for who I was.

So I asked myself a different question: *What would be fun or cool about publishing this book?*

I thought about the essays I'd published in magazines, and the one I'd just sold to the *New York Times*, and about how much I enjoyed working with the editors. I thought about how I'd liked the help I got from that small publisher with my last book, how they'd made it better with their efforts. I liked the idea of having a team on my side, and the collaborative nature of publishing. Working with the publishing house, that would be the actual *experience* of selling the book, and that was something I believed I would enjoy.

That Monday I heard from the agent again. A publisher was *very* interested. So interested, they made an offer a couple weeks later.

Did the publisher make an offer *because* I'd gotten clear about why I wanted to publish it? I don't know. But I do know that just as I can't write a story while wondering what other people will think of it, I also can't accomplish anything, achieve anything, complete anything that I hope will prove my worth. I will find a way to mess that up every time.

I don't think I am unique. It is easier sometimes to know why we write. Writing as an experience is immediately gratifying. To get into that creative flow, to get connected to what feeds me my ideas, is to feel a purpose. Life does not get better than that. Period. As I have said, I can experience that creative flow doing other things, but regardless of how I experience it, for me that effortless, present flow state is life as it is meant to be lived. So it is not hard to know why I write. I do it for that experience, as does every writer I know. The experience alone is all the reason I really need.

It gets more complicated with publishing. Publishing something is a result. It's actually more than that, but as an ex-sprinter, I know it can look an awful lot like a finish line, what you lean across to see which color ribbon you'll claim. There are so many aspects to publishing that are measurable, from the size of the publisher, to the amount of the advance, to the number of sales, to the bestseller ranking that are not themselves experiences but are tempting opportunities to measure oneself. The temptation is so great, in fact, that it subconsciously keeps many people, myself included, from publishing their work.

This is why it is so important to get clear about why we publish what we write. Here are my reasons. Yours might be a little different, but if I know anything about writers, they probably won't be all that different.

First, as I said, I like the collaborative nature of working with a publisher. I like the back and forth with the editor and having someone copyedit my work, having someone bring their creative powers to the cover design, and having a sales team representing it to bookstores. I like having a team gathered together briefly to put this baby out into the world. The support I receive from that team feels like the support I feel from the creative flow when I'm really in it, reminding me I can trust other people just as I have learned to trust the source of that flow.

But perhaps you enjoy self-publishing. I know people who do. From my limited experience of it, I can understand why. There is a pleasure in making all those decisions, of being in charge of the production of the book the way a director is in charge of a movie set. The successful published indie authors I know are happy little businesspeople, hiring cover designers and copyeditors and publicists, working social media, and promoting their work at conferences. They'll often talk about the money, how they aren't giving up the lion's share of their earnings to a corporation in New York, but the truth is, these people like being in charge. It's fun for them, and so that's what they do, and that's why they do it well.

Which brings me to the second reason I like to publish my work: the money. To be clear, I never started writing because I thought it was the best way to get rich quick. If it's money you want, become an investment banker or a lawyer or a plastic surgeon. Though I do know plenty of authors who make a good living writing, and a few who make a fantastic living. It's important to remember this is possible because there's a lot of hand-wringing in the writing community about how much money we make—or, more specifically, how much money we don't. I will not contribute to that gloomy chorus.

I will not contribute to it because I *love* the money I make writing. Not specifically the *amount*, but simply the money itself, the fact that I am paid to do this thing that I would and, God knows, *have* happily done for free. Every time I get paid for an essay or a book or a lecture or a workshop associated with my writing, I am reminded that I need not divide my life into work and pleasure. I have spent many years living for a theoretical weekend, that moment when my time will finally be mine. Money was always the single greatest obstacle to that freedom. I needed a certain amount of it simply to survive, and for a long time, like most people, I did what I could to earn it, toiling away while dreaming of a different life.

Mere survival is a low and depressing motivator. It's not a frame of mind in which I want to dwell. It's a fearful, greedy, and suspicious way to live. Love is the greatest motivator I know. When I deposit a check I received from something I loved writing and loved sharing, I am reminded that there is no real separation between the body and spirit, that the latter can support the former. That is freedom, if I can remember it.

Love is the greatest motivator I know.

The third reason I love to publish my work is for the conversation. Writing at its core *is* a conversation. It's a conversation I'm having with myself and with my readers. I first truly understood this when I published an essay in the *New York Times* called "No One Is Broken" about the most valuable lesson I learned raising Jack. The feedback was great, and as I read the comments and replied to e-mails, I thought, This *is the conversation I want to have. I want to talk about how no one is broken, how everyone's good enough, and everyone has what it takes.* There were so many other things I could talk about, from politics to games to sex to science to religion, all of which were interesting in their own ways, but if I had to choose the conversation that absolutely interested me most, it would be about how everyone is good enough already.

Publishing a book or an essay gives me an opportunity to have the kind of conversations I most want to have. It doesn't matter what kind of book you write. If you write dystopian science fiction, then you almost certainly love to talk about dystopian science fiction. If you love poetry, you love to talk about poetry. I love talking to writers about the emotional challenges of writing more than, say, the nitty-gritty of craft. The books and essays I've written reflect this interest, so that when people contact me to teach at their conference or speak to their writing organization, they do so because they, too, want to have this conversation. It's a win-win.

The conversations I have about my work happen in many ways. Sometimes I have them in interviews I do, sometimes in the workshops I teach and with the clients I work with, and sometimes through e-mails and social media. But that conversation also happens without my immediate participation. After I published that collection of essays, I was doing a signing at a bookstore in Spokane. A woman approached the signing table with her copy of the book, and as I readied my pen, she said, "Can I show you something?" She pulled out her phone and showed me a photo. "That's a picture of where I write. You see that quote I've got pinned to the wall?"

I squinted. "Hey, that looks familiar. Did I write that?"

"Yes! That's what I look at every day when I write."

While it was flattering that this woman used something I'd written as a daily motivation, what *I* found most inspiring about seeing the quote was the understanding that my book, in its own way, was having a conversation without me. I know this not just because of what readers tell me, but because of what I go through when I read something, how a story will get me thinking or upset me or give me a new idea. If I never meet that author, their work will still be a part of a conversation I am having with myself, and with other people, and with life itself. I will know only the smallest fraction of the conversations my work has been a part of, and yet I am glad those conversations are happening and for anything I contributed to them.

Which brings me to the last and most mysterious of the reasons I publish my work: *discovery.* I often have to remind myself that the most interesting part of *being* in The Flow is the discovery, that I don't actually know what I'm going to write and that I don't *want* to know what I'm going to write. Even though I write about my own life and my own experiences, I am always surprised by what I find in my writing. I must remind myself that I like this discovery because it means being comfortable with the unknown. I can't discover something I already know. To write happily, I must get comfortable with not knowing and then discovering, and then with not knowing again and then discovering again.

The same is true with sharing my work. I was surprised how publishing a collection of essays with a tiny publisher with no marketing budget and no sales team still opened up many opportunities for me. Some of those opportunities, like bookstore appearances and teaching at conferences, I pursued, but many others came to me on their own. Sometimes those opportunities were lectures or clients or interviews, and sometimes they were simply meeting people I would not have met otherwise.

To write a book is to take a journey to discover how that book will begin and end, and to publish that book is to take yet another journey with just as much discovery. And just as in my writing, my favorite aspects of this journey are the parts I didn't plan, didn't set up myself, the experiences that surprised me. Oh, how I've believed I never wanted to be surprised by *anything*, have thought the safest and best route is one planned and known the way I used to know my way to work, driving on the same roads and freeways and parking in the same spot every night. Yet the greatest feeling of safety I have known in my life is when I accepted what I couldn't know or plan and have instead gotten curious about what is to come. Now I am safe right where I stand and my eyes are on the road and I am interested in where I'm going, which is always where I want to be.

CHAPTER TWELVE

Gatekeepers

As of this writing, the world of independent publishing, or self-publishing, has exploded with the advent of digital technology. It's simply much cheaper and easier to design and distribute indie books through online platforms than it was before the Internet existed. I know a few people who've had some success publishing their own stuff. Most of them are romance writers, but a few are nonfiction authors. All of them are also entrepreneurs of sorts, or at least the kinds of people who would build their own deck or install their own garbage disposal. They like doing things themselves, micromanaging others, and are not at all fatigued by the amount of work that has nothing whatsoever to do with writing that is required to create their mini one-author publishing company.

I am not one of those people, nor, I have come to understand, are the majority of the authors choosing to self-publish their work. Most of them chose to self-publish because of what we have come to call gatekeepers. These are the agents, editors, and sales teams that have to say yes to a book before it can appear in a bookstore. Combined, these people will say no to a lot of books—far, far more than they will say yes to.

I hope I'm not telling you anything you don't already know. I take no pleasure in being the bearer of what sounds like bad news. However, if this is the first time you're learning this, do not despair. And if this is not the first time you've learned this, if you've learned it again and again and again before as I have, you shouldn't despair, either. No one should self-publish a book simply because they dislike the experience of dealing with gatekeepers, of trying to unravel the mystery of why these people say yes to one book and no to another. Self-publish because you like doing things yourself. Do not self-publish because you can't figure out how to unlock those gates.

Before I go any further, I want you to know that you already possess the key to those gates. You've always had it. As annoying as that may be to hear, it's critical you understand it, far more important than knowing the reality of rejection rates. As with anything you already possess, the time spent looking for it will be confusing and circular and probably disappointing. If your house keys are in your pocket, and you search every drawer in your home for them, you will conclude they are lost. I will not, however, name that key just yet. I'm not being coy. Giving its name out of context can make the key seem obtuse and just as frustrating as all those rejection letters.

You may find it just as frustrating as the very, very good advice I've given my son Jack about dating. When he was twenty, he realized he wanted a girlfriend. He wanted a girl-friend about as much as he wanted anything else. Jack, as I've mentioned, did not come at life the way a lot of other people have. We had to start homeschooling him when he was twelve because his experiences in traditional school were becoming chaotic. Prior to that, he rarely chose to socialize with other kids. He put himself into a kind of bubble where, as he explained to me much later, he would "not be influenced by others." He didn't want to be influenced by other kids, teachers, nor, apparently, his parents.

All of which led to a young man with underdeveloped social skills. To be clear, Jack developed *other* skills while not socializing, the kinds of skills people often learn while going through a midlife crisis, the skills of imagination and of dreaming and of listening to one's own ideas. There is no enduring happiness without these, but they alone cannot fully replace the nuanced socializing skills most of us learn in school and at home, skills I continue to learn to this day.

And nowhere are those tools more necessary than dating, or, in Jack's case, simply talking to girls. He and I would drive to a nearby Barnes & Noble and get some coffee and cookies and talk about life—well, *his* life anyway—and he'd complain about his plight. No girl would be interested in him. He's a weirdo. Also, girls were confusing. What did they want? They weren't like him. They seemed like a different species.

So, I'd give him advice. After all, I'd had some experience in this department. I'd dated many girls before I married his mother. I knew the difference between being with someone I loved and being with someone I just thought was attractive. I knew the difference between trying to impress a girl, trying to get a girl's attention, trying to be cool, and actually being— not *trying* to be, but actually *being*—interested in someone.

"You're coming at this backward," I told him. "By the way, everyone does. I certainly did once upon a time. But it's still backward. You shouldn't be asking what do girls want in a guy, you should be asking, 'What do *I* want in a girlfriend? Who's interesting to *me*? Who's attractive to *me*?'"

His answer to these questions the first time I asked them— and the second and third and fourth time—was the same as I have heard given by grown men who supposedly have social skills, who have jobs and friends and have never been told they are on any kind of spectrum: *I like girls who like me.* In other words, I don't care. I just want a girlfriend who will say yes to me.

Why do writers need to hear this? Because I had a very hard time getting an agent for either of my first two novels. When I finally did find agents, they were not very good and they sent my manuscript to only a couple publishing houses before abandoning the book. Things went differently for my third novel. First, I wrote it differently. I found a very cool story and a voice that suited me. It was set in the 1880s, and I actually did the research necessary to make it realistic. As it happens, about the same time I finished it I attended a writers' conference where I could pitch to agents. I found one who seemed promising, made my appointment, and showed up bright-eyed and caffeinated that morning.

I liked her right away. She was a little older, which I preferred, and had a nice sense of humor. After I gave my pitch we chatted easily, and she told me she'd become an agent because she liked working with writers. She said she wanted to see the whole manuscript. I sent it (by mail; this was in the late nineties) on the Monday after the conference. Exactly a week later I came home and found a message on my answering machine from her. She wanted to talk. I called her and she told me she had picked up my manuscript after having gotten only four hours of sleep the night before and yet she couldn't put it down. "It's a great story," she said.

Happy day! I had an agent. An actual, legitimate agent. She returned my e-mails and my phone calls. She laughed at my jokes. She'd be sending it out to all the major houses right away. So it began. Be patient, she told me. For a time, I could be. When I felt low, I'd just remember that I had an agent and things were happening. Molly, the agent, was like a life preserver. If I began to drown in self-doubt, I'd remember I had an agent, which was proof that someone wanted what I was offering. I started my next novel. She *loved* its title. When the first rejections from the publishing houses came in, she told me not to worry. Most of them were complimentary, and the editors said they would be interested in seeing something else from me. "If not this one, then the next one," she said. This was good. We were in this together. When I sent her the first two chapters for the new novel, she called to tell me how *brilliant* they were. "Where do you get these *ideas*?" she asked.

The day finally came that we had to admit the first novel wasn't going to be bought. It was disappointing, but Molly looked forward to reading the final version of this next book. I wrote and wrote and sent it her way. A week later the e-mail came. She didn't understand it. What's the story about? It doesn't come together. She couldn't represent it.

I was devastated. I was reminded of my own junior high school days, when I'd first started dating. In those days, most of the girls I asked out either said no or dumped me. Dumped. That's just what had happened with Molly, I thought. I felt exactly as I had when I was twelve and thirteen and fourteen and a girl had dumped me—unwanted and rejected.

All the while this drama with my agent was unfolding, something else was afoot. Another waiter at the restaurant where I was working told me he played Dungeons & Dragons. I'd been playing this game since its inception in the seventies. I played it as a kid and off and on as an adult. I was always what is called the Dungeon Master, or the DM, the one who invented the stories, the adventures, for the game. This waiter told me he'd published an adventure he'd written in a magazine called *Dungeon*, which was published by TSR, the company responsible for D&D. "They paid you for it?" I asked. "Five hundred dollars," he said.

Literary magazines would often pay in one free copy. I loved D&D and had always thought I'd like to publish an adventure. I bought a copy of the magazine and read it through. I *never* bought copies of the literary magazines I submitted to. I thought I could definitely write an adventure as good as those I'd read, and wrote up a pitch and sent it in. A few weeks later I got a rejection.

I complained to my wife. I don't know how to pitch to these people, I said. I don't know what they want. I have no other ideas. "What about all that stuff you're designing for your friends? Isn't there something in there?" She was referring to the adventures I spent an hour or so most days dreaming up for that waiter and his pals. It hadn't occurred to me to use something I'd designed *just for fun*. In my mind, there seemed to be a difference between what you did for fun and what you did for profit. *Why not?* I thought. I picked something in the big adventure I was designing that was short enough for the magazine and sent the idea in. A couple weeks later I got the reply. They wanted me to write it.

It was disorienting. It had been so easy. I immediately stopped working on my latest novel and spent the next few weeks writing the adventure. I loved writing it. Suddenly, this thing I'd been doing for fun, this thing I liked thinking about simply because it was easy to think about, suddenly it was something else, something professional, something *real*. I finished it and sent it in and it was accepted. I signed a contract. I got a check. And several months later I received my copy of the magazine.

When I opened it and found my adventure, I thought, *This is the single coolest thing I have ever seen in my entire life. I want everything I write to be published.* I loved the experience of seeing what had been inside of me outside of me. I loved the experience of seeing it translated into this other form, of seeing the maps I'd made by my hand redrawn by their artists, of seeing the artwork drawn by their artists that accompanied it. And I loved that somewhere someone was going to play this adventure, was going to have fun with it, this thing I'd dreamed to have fun playing myself.

Because that was how I dreamed adventures. I thought,

What would be fun to do? If there was one thing I knew how to do it was have fun. If you don't know how to have fun, what *can* you know how to do? So, I'd sit and think about fun until something fun came to me and then I'd write it down and run my friends through it, and they'd say, "That was fun!" That's how you win at Dungeons & Dragons, by the way. You have fun. No winners or losers. The point of the game is to have fun.

I came up with another idea, a longer one, and the editor wanted that one as well. By this time, I was starting to develop a new idea of what a published adventure could be. I felt like the adventures TSR published fell into a predictable pattern. I wanted something different. I wanted the players to have a sense of discovery, to feel as though *they* were responsible for the adventure, not the Dungeon Master. I wanted the players to know how important their choices were. I started implementing this theory with my friends. Surely, I could do the same for the adventures that I would publish again and again in *Dungeon*.

I wrote up a proposal for this new kind of adventure and sent it off to the editor, whom I had met by this time. He liked the idea. I dove in and wrote it up. A few weeks later he sent it back. Not for him. Didn't feel like a *real* adventure.

Screw him, I thought. *Screw* Dungeon *magazine. He's wrong. This* is *cool.* I knew it was cool because when I played it with my friends it was cool. I never sent another idea to him.

About six months later I was in the restaurant again when the wine steward showed me something. It was a D&D module, which is an adventure published in the form of its own little book. "Don't you do this sort of thing?" he said.

"I do. Where'd you get it?"

"This guy, my regular—he says he just published it."

"He published *this*?"

"Yeah."

"I need to talk to him."

So, I did. His name was also Bill, and he was about my age and had been playing D&D as long as I had. He was incredibly high energy and not really what I thought of as a typical D&D player—meaning my gamer-radar, something you need when you're looking for other people to play with, would never have picked him out of a crowd. He was unapologetically passionate about the game. Standing there in the restaurant, I told him, "I need to write for you."

He said, "Well, send me an idea." I said I would. I sat down and banged out my vision of a new kind of adventure. I got a call from him a couple days later. He loved it. He wanted me to write it for him.

"Great," I said. This did not surprise me at all. In my mind, he had already told me he wanted it, even though he hadn't.

"Bill," he said. "You understand our publishing company— we don't publish other people. So far, we've only published my stuff. You're our first writer who I've thought even came close to offering us something we'd want to put our name on."

"Oh. Okay. Cool."

"So—you're the first."

"Right. Got it. When do you want the manuscript?"

So began my relationship writing for Necromancer Games. I wrote two long book-length adventures and contributed to another Bill was working on. Both of my adventures actually won awards for Best Adventure of the Year. To this day, those are the only writing awards I've ever won. Writing them was effortless. All I needed was time, which I had enough of.

And then, after the second book-length adventure, I was done. The money wasn't great, and I wasn't feeling inspired any longer. I knew I wanted to focus more on my other writing, that there was something in that writing that needed my full attention. For years afterward, Bill would call me every so often asking for more adventures. I found myself in the odd position of saying no, again and again, to a publisher.

Technically, Bill was a gatekeeper. I did not perceive him as such. As soon as I met him, I recognized him as a kind of friend, a gamer-friend, specifically—but a friend just the same. A friend is like someone headed in the same direction as I am. We want the same things, more or less, and it will be easier to get what we want if we do it together. My current agent is a friend, too. I needed a new agent and someone recommended her. I called her and we had a long chat and got along very well. As it happens, she wants to sell books and I want my books to sell, so we have that in common, but we have many other things in common as well, things that have nothing to do with books.

And my wife is a friend also. When I met her many years ago, I recognized something in her I didn't quite realize I was looking for. She and I were and still are headed in the same direction, are having the same conversation about life and how best to live it, about why we suffer and why we don't. I have never grown tired of that conversation.

The key, as you have probably intuited, is love—but let me

be specific. Just as you don't want to write just any book, or marry just any person, so too you don't want to sign with just any agent or just any publisher. I know very, very well what it is to think, *I don't care who publishes my book, I just want* someone *to publish it!* I have had this thought many times. But it's dishonest. I want to write the book I most want to write, and I want to find the publisher who most wants to publish it, who is as excited by it as I am, who sees in it the same potential I see. I want an agent and a publisher who want to take part in the conversation I want to have. If they don't want to have that conversation, then we should not be together. I want my agent and publisher to be my book friends.

The only way to find those friends is to pay attention to the conversation I want to have. That conversation is within me. It is known to me as my dreams are known to me. Publishing a book is a kind of dream, really. It starts in a place where no one else can see it, is real to only one person at first. You dream it and dream it until you can see it on the page. Agents and editors, meanwhile, dream of publishing books. Like you, they want these books to sell many, many copies, but they also want to publish books they love, dreaming of being a part of bringing something beautiful into the world. And readers are looking for the dream of a book as well. They want to go on that dream journey, have that dream conversation about love or wizards and elves or cops and killers.

In this way, a book is born when all these dreams overlap. Do not worry about what other people are dreaming. You dream your dream. It *will* lead you to the people it needs, the same way the dream of the story came to you. You didn't *make* that book; you invited it into your life. It came to you and you followed it. Trust it to help you find its friends the same way you trusted it to teach you how to write it. There are no gates. There are only people, like you, looking for the conversations they want to have, looking for what they love.

CHAPTER THIRTEEN

The Hard Part

This is the part of the book where I must remind you that writing is both a craft and a business. Though I am far more interested in talking to writers about how they feel while they write or how they feel when they pitch their books at writers' conferences, and how everyone is born with the perfect equipment necessary to write the book they most want to write—the truth is, no one is born knowing how to write, and absolutely no one is born knowing about the business of publishing. All that has to be learned. As Flannery O'Conner said, "Everyone knows what a story is until they try to write one."

I have spent the last thirty or so years learning how to tell stories and, eventually, learning how to sell those stories to other people. The more I learned, the better things went. As I have mentioned, this learning involved a lot of disappointment and rejection. It involved thousands of hours crafting stories that no one bought, that hardly anyone would read. No one assigned me those hours; I was not paid for them nor were they logged in any classroom. Had I stopped writing, nothing in the world would have changed. I went to my desk every day despite the rejections, despite midnight terrors, despite feeling at times as if I couldn't find my stories.

As I have said, this went on for about twenty years. Twenty years is a very long time when you think about it. And I mean that literally—it was long *when* I thought about it, which I often did. I'd think, *Jesus All Mighty, I've been at this for ten years, fifteen years,* twenty *years, and look where I am!* On the other hand, when I wasn't thinking about it, it wasn't long at all. When I wasn't thinking about it, I was just living another day. The problem was, I thought about it with every rejection, every birthday, every new book; I started hoping, *This will be the one.*

Sounds kind of horrible, doesn't it? Sounds hard, in fact. It often was. So much of what I experienced in those twenty years I never want to experience again. But I am not the sort of writer who likes to tell other writers how hard this life can be. That feels like bragging to me. On the other hand, to cheer you up, I could tell you about the writers I know who published their very first book, their very first story even, who did not spend years and years in the writing desert. There's a bunch of them. Maybe you'll be one; maybe you are one.

Except that won't help with the hard part, either. All that will help with the hard part is learning. Whether you publish the first book you wrote or the fifteenth book you wrote, you're going to have to learn the craft and business of writing. You're going to have to learn about beginnings, middles, and endings; about characters and tension; about what makes a good sentence and what makes a sloppy sentence. And you're going to have to learn about agents and editors and marketing and platforms. How fast this learning occurs depends entirely on you, on whether you allow your mind to be open or closed to the learning you need. It is not always so easy to be open to that learning.

I did not fully understand my role in what I learned or did not learn until my wife, Jen, and I homeschooled Jack. Or, I should say, we *tried* to homeschool Jack. Most of what we did with him did not look anything like school. What it looked like was watching documentaries, going for walks, listening to music, and having long conversations about the individual and society; it also looked like arguments and doors slamming and tears. There was very little sitting quietly and writing essays, or solving math problems, or reading about the Constitution, or doing science experiments in the kitchen.

The problem was Jack—but I'm not blaming him! I simply mean that he taught me that there can be no school without a student's willing participation. Jack showed up physically every day for our classes, but on most days his mind was elsewhere. Everything we did, all our unconventional and largely ineffective methods, were attempts to attract Jack's attention, to entice him to bring his mind to class. In the end, nothing a teacher says or does will have any effect unless the student chooses to give them his attention, in the same way an author's story cannot reach their reader unless that reader turns her attention to the words on the page, stops thinking about her chores and children and job, and allows the story into her mind. I have found myself reading books and realized that for two paragraphs I've lost track of the story, that I've been more or less reciting the words in my mind while I thought about something else.

This is what I must have been doing when I was being taught grammar in junior high school. Because I read a lot, and because my parents spoke in full sentences, most of what I wrote was grammatically correct, though I could not tell you why. I couldn't diagram a sentence, and I couldn't tell you what a predicate was, or what a subject or an object was—nor did I want to. Those were just a bunch of rules dreamed up by people without imaginations who needed those rules to do anything and who never just did something because it felt right. *Screw your rules*, I thought, *I have a story to tell.*

Except by the time I was halfway through my second novel, I realized I wasn't entirely 100 percent clear where a comma belonged or didn't belong, and sometimes I'd get a little confused about tense, and sometimes a sentence seemed off and I couldn't figure out why, and I secretly suspected it had something to do with those rules. This didn't happen often, though, and I didn't spend a lot of time worrying about it because I was creating art, after all, and sometimes art breaks rules.

But sometimes I was writing letters to agents and editors, and those letters *weren't* art, and one day I was banging one of those out and I reached a moment where I was trying to figure out if my sentence needed a comma, and I realized that whether I put it in or not felt like a guess. I thought how I didn't want to give an agent any reason to stop reading my query letter. A couple of silly grammatical mistakes could be just such a reason.

As it happens, I had recently attended a writers' conference and sat in on a class on grammar. And "sat in" is apparently all I did because I remembered nothing about that class except that I liked the teacher. She was energetic and bright and had a nice sense of humor. I had also gotten her card because she offered her services as a proofreader. I called her and told her I wanted a grammar lesson. I told her I'd bring her something I'd written and that I wanted her to go through it and point out every mistake I'd made and why I'd made it and what the rules were and how to follow them.

I showed up to her house for my lesson ready to learn. It was a great lesson, though I only learned two things. First, I learned about what is called the Oxford comma, or the serial comma, and I have been an adherent to it ever since. That is the only grammar rule I learned that day, though in teaching it to me I learned something else, something far more valuable that would improve my grammar from that day forward.

"You see," she explained, "if you write, 'Every Tom, Dick, and Harry' and *don't* put a comma after 'Dick,' then you're sort of combining Dick and Harry, making them one entity, as if Tom is one thing, and DickandHarry is another thing."

"I get it," I said.

What I was getting, in addition to the comma thing, is that the reason you needed that second comma was not because it was a rule (and if you know anything about the history of commas, you know that some people do *not* follow this rule—do not even recognize it as a rule), but because it made the sentence clearer. *That* was the most important lesson I learned about grammar that day: that punctuation and tense and proper sentence structure were not just a bunch of rules to be followed, but were instead tools to help the reader understand what was being written. Punctuation marks, in particular, were like signposts and stage directions for a sentence, often mimicking the pauses and emphasis in speech.

This may seem obvious to you, but it wasn't to me. Yet as soon as I saw grammar in this light, my relationship to it changed. I didn't give a damn about grammar as a concept, but I *did* care about clarity. I still can't diagram a sentence and I might not be able to name an object and a subject, but I have become very fussy about my commas and em dashes and ellipses and parentheses; I am as fussy and particular about the punctuation as the words I choose.

This lesson immediately improved my overall writing, but it didn't help much with those letters to agents and editors. Though they were now grammatically correct, I still found query letters odious and awkward. Every time I finished one, no matter how many times I rewrote it, polished it, read it aloud to my wife and asked her what she thought, I still felt like I'd gotten it wrong, that it was missing something and that it was ultimately ineffective. My results from those letters echoed this belief. I knew they weren't awful. I was a skilled enough writer, and I knew about making sure the agent actually represented the kind of story I was sending, and about mentioning the other books they'd sold in the first paragraph, and about how long the letter should be; but the rejections far,

far outweighed the requests for material, and I knew the problem was in that letter.

I knew it because whenever I pitched my books at conferences I always—every-single-time always—was asked to send something. I got so frustrated with this dynamic that I actually hired someone to help me write better queries. She taught me about making sure there was conflict within the description of the story, which helped a little, but still didn't solve the mystery of what was actually missing.

I never did solve that mystery while I was querying agents. The agents I got came via conferences or recommendations from other writers. It wasn't until I wrote my first book proposal that I understood what was missing from all those query letters.

While I found the queries awkward, I initially found the idea of a book proposal obnoxious. If you're not familiar, a proposal is like a little business plan for your nonfiction book. It includes a description of the book's concept, what makes it different from similar books, a chapter-by-chapter outline, samples chapters, comparable titles, a marketplace evaluation, a marketing plan, a description of your platform, and endorsements from authors and experts. As a former fiction writer, I thought this was an enormous waste of time. Why not just read the book? And don't the agents and editors know all that marketplace stuff?

These are perfectly good questions, but not if you want to sell a book, which I did. Once I was done griping about the state of publishing, I sat down and began my first proposal. Fortunately, I was quite passionate about that particular project. I'd been writing about it and talking about it for several years. I always enjoyed an opportunity to talk to anyone about it—at parties, at conferences, on the street. I was only about two paragraphs into the proposal when I realized I didn't feel like I was trying to manufacture what I hoped would be an acceptable bit of salesmanship; I was actually enjoying myself. I was enjoying myself for the same reason I always enjoyed myself when I turned my attention to this book's subject. The proposal, I understood, was just another way to talk about the book, only to talk about it in a way that included the question: *Do you, agent or editor, want to talk about this some more?*

Now I could *learn* how to write a proposal. Now I was interested in the form and could bring my enthusiasm and creativity to it the same as I brought my enthusiasm and creativity to the actual book. I could do that because I understood the proposal's value beyond merely selling. I understood it as an actual form of honest communication rather than manipulation and hucksterism. Now I could be myself.

I love to learn, as do most people. I can enjoy the very act of it, even when it's something in which I'm not deeply interested. It's always easier to learn, however, when I actually want what the learning will bring me. The first thing I ever learned how to cook on my own were pancakes. I was ten, and pancakes were just about my favorite food. I was tired of waiting for my mother to agree to make them for me, so I asked her to show me how. I absorbed that lesson with the hunger of a boy ready for breakfast. Oh, the freedom! I have since mastered the pancake, in my opinion. I made them for my boys, who have never asked me how to make them. They were not as passionate about the pancake as I.

Now that we're done homeschooling Jack, now that he's a little older and more reflective, we talk often about his time in public school and what it was like for him. He sometimes regrets he didn't stick it out, that he wasn't able to get a traditional degree. Yet he also says that while he was in school, he didn't see the point in paying attention to what his teachers wanted him to pay attention to. None of it seemed fun or interesting and he didn't understand how learning this stuff would help him in the future.

This made perfect sense to me. I quit college when I no longer saw the point in any of it. I've sometimes regretted that choice, dreaming about how much easier my life would have been if I'd just gotten my degree. But I couldn't. I couldn't make myself believe I needed to learn what was being taught. I do not mean to suggest there is no point in college. My wife has two undergraduate degrees. Most of my friends have degrees. Just about everyone I know who has a degree is glad they have it. Yet simply having a degree wasn't enough motivation for me to put in the time necessary to acquire one, so I left and started learning on my own.

Learn I did, but I struggled mightily for many years because it took me that long to learn that I had to write for pleasure and not profit. Once I wrote for pleasure, the profits came. Once I wrote for pleasure, the craft improved as well because I wanted that much more to make clear, to share, what my pleasure brought me. And once I wrote for pleasure, I was more eager to learn *how* to share that work, to market it, to give other people the opportunity to take part in this conversation I very much wanted to have.

Without pleasure, I don't know what the point of anything is. Without pleasure, I want to crawl into my bed and go to sleep forever. The only thing I've ever wanted in my life is to be happy, to enjoy myself, to play. I have mistaken where that pleasure comes from. For a time, I believed that success would lift some weight that suppressed pleasure, as if my happiness would arrive after I had completed a great assignment. Until that time, my happiness was waiting for me in some eternal weekend, when the school of struggle and achievement would finally be over, for I had *made it* and could say that I no longer had anything to prove because at last I knew I was good enough, and now I could just enjoy myself.

That's what I believed all those years I was struggling and, oh, life was often hard. Everything was hard. Writing was hard, querying was hard, rejection was hard. *When would it get easier?* I wanted to know. I dreamed of that time. I fantasized about success, imagining the ease of it, the bliss of not caring, of having nothing to prove, of simply being enough as I was. Strange I could imagine it as if it were real, that I could picture this reality with the same clarity with which I wrote my stories, and yet I believed the portal into that reality was somehow in other people's hands.

If you want to be a professional writer, then you must learn all that is necessary, and you can. You can learn from books and conferences and workshops and, of course, from simply doing it. You will learn from rejections and acceptance letters, from stories that work and stories that don't work. But your learning will be slowed by the degree to which you fear you might be wasting your time. If you feel some people have what it takes and some do not, if you worry some mornings that you are one of those who does not have what it takes, then you will not see the point in learning anything. You can't learn your way into having what it takes. You can only learn how to use what you have always had.

You can't learn your way into having what it takes.

If you worry you don't have what it takes, then even the pleasure you take finding the right sentence, the pleasure you take falling into the dream of the story you're telling, will seem ultimately valueless, a thing with which to amuse yourself when you can't think of something better and more profitable to do. To believe your own pleasure, your own joy, your own excitement and enthusiasm have no meaning in and of themselves is to believe that your life has no meaning. It is the darkest thought we can let creep into our mind, a thought that drains all creativity out of our days. Our pleasure is the light that guides us through our stories and lives, letting us know we're headed in our right direction. To ignore that light is to cast yourself willingly into the darkness of despair and failure.

No matter how many times I cast myself into that very hole, I was still incapable of wanting to feel anything but good. I couldn't change that if I wanted to. No matter how much I dreamed of the ease and pleasure I would know when I'd found success in the future, I could not turn off the desire to feel good in the present moment. No matter how conditional I believe my happiness and well-being may be, no matter how sure I am that I must have published *these* many books, or received these kinds of reviews, or won that kind of award, or lived in this kind of house, or driven that kind of car to simply be allowed to feel good, I cannot stop wanting to feel happy and content every single moment of every single day. It's never-ending. The moment I accept this, learning and writing and publishing and living itself gets much easier.

CHAPTER FOURTEEN

Fame

M y father went back to school in his forties to learn computer programming. This was in the late seventies and early eighties, when computers were becoming something a person might actually have in their home, rather than monolithic walls of blinking lights in temperature-controlled rooms in NASA and the Pentagon. This was also the same time I entered high school, when I had begun to cast my thoughts out into the future of my adulthood, testing what I might like to do with myself when I was a grown-up. Though I'd gone to a high school with an arts "magnet program" specifically to study creative writing, I was still young enough to be open to other possibilities.

One August day I was sitting in the back seat of our family car as my mother drove my brother, sister, and I out of muggy Providence toward the breezy relief of Horse Neck Beach. Being driven somewhere was a great opportunity for daydreaming. My mind drifted as I watched the office towers and traffic lights of the city recede and the verdant summer green of rural Rhode Island speed past. I thought of what my father had shown me recently about how to program in BASIC, how the if-this-then-that nature of it reminded me a bit of the Dungeons & Dragons adventures I was designing for my friends. I thought how programming was sort of like a cross between math and writing, that you were creating streams of logical thought, and how you could get an actual job doing it, and how nice it would be to be paid to do something that was at least a little creative. For a moment, I was able to picture myself as a computer engineer, a logical problem-solver, a man with a briefcase and a desk and a job to do.

"Maybe I'll be a computer programmer," I said aloud. Sometimes simply speaking an idea is an easy way to test whether you're actually interested in it.

"Sure," said my mom. "I'd bet you'd make a great programmer."

"Yeah," I replied. "Yeah, maybe . . ."

I could already feel the steam leaking out of that plan. If I was programmer, how would I ever be famous?

This was and remained a very real consideration of mine. Fame and artistic success seemed inextricably linked: The former was how you knew you were the latter. What's more, I'd spent most of my life watching, listening to, and reading about famous people. Their names and deeds were part of the common vocabulary, like literal stars visible to all from their proximity above us. To be able to shine your light so bright everyone could see it seemed more than a worthy goal; it seemed like the very best goal. It meant you were your full self, that you had not dimmed what you could offer the world, that you were doing more than your part to light what had grown dark from doubt, fear, and inattention. That people also screamed your name and paid you lots of money for this light was just a happy bonus.

When I was a senior, I hosted our high school's morning radio program, reading the news before tossing it to Janet for the weather and Carl for sports. Early in the year, my producer created a funny opening for the show: A door was heard opening and closing, followed by a set of footsteps clacking along a floor before stopping abruptly. A man's voice then declared, "Huh! It's Bill Kenower!"

That's what played every single morning before the show. I was perfectly okay with it. Once I passed a kid in the hall who looked a year or two younger than I, whom I'd never met, and this kid called out, "Hey! You Bill Kenower?"

"Yes," I replied. "Yes, I am."

I was bartending in my early twenties when my brother and I were also performing a sketch comedy show around Providence. One day a young guy came in to get some lunch and he noticed me. "You're that guy from *The American Basement Review*, aren't you?"

"That's right."

"Yeah, I really liked that show. I liked that one line you said about feeling like the world's smallest peanut in the world's largest shell."

No one had ever quoted a line of mine back to me. I stood

for a moment behind the bar in Montana Restaurant, watching as the guy recited the line again softly to himself, nodding in the way you do when you're rolling something over in your mind. I noticed how when he said it, the line sounded different than how it sounded to me when I wrote it or even when I'd spoken it on stage, that he had turned it into something of his own. It struck me that something I'd dreamed had rippled out into the heart of a stranger, and that if he hadn't come into the restaurant, I'd have no more known its effect on him than what someone was having for breakfast in China. It also struck me that there was nothing more to say to him about it, that it was a strange way to relate to someone, that this person was in that moment more interested in me than I really was in him. It was like talking to a girl as I realized she had a crush on me: flattering but uncomfortable.

I received one piece of fan mail for that show. It had been sent to the theater where we were performing the A.B.R. for the last time. I read it backstage while our lighting guy was setting up. The letter's author thanked me for the show and quoted scripture and talked about the light of God she felt within the show. It was a nice letter, but I sensed she wasn't even writing to me, that she was instead writing to herself, that seeing the show had reminded her of something, and she had to share what she had remembered with someone. Sitting with that letter, I thought how the kind of fame I dreamed about would just be this times a million, all these strangers not knowing me but feeling connected to something for which I was responsible. No—not even responsible. The show just seemed like a door I'd opened. Anyone could have opened it, it wasn't my door, I'd just noticed it and said, "Hey! Everyone. Look at this!"

My wife observed that if that show had been as successful as my brother and I had initially hoped it would be, if we'd kept doing it, if we'd gone to New York or Chicago or Los Angeles and it had taken off there, I might not have survived. I was already smoking too much pot to manage the stress and velocity of energy doing the show generated in me. I'll never know what would have happened, but I do believe you get whatever you're ready to receive.

Jen mentioned how challenging early success might have been for me when I was a few years into my time at the restaurant and starting to feel a little antsy from the lack of achievement and attention and approval. The antsiness would get worse. All those years I spent waiting tables while I wrote my novels were like time spent in a desert for a man thirsty for fame and success. It's hard to be less famous than being a waiter, I thought. It got so bad I noticed one day that I often had a play-by-play announcer talking in my head, praising everything I did from changing lanes on the freeway to tossing a tableside Caesar salad. It was as if without someone noticing what I was doing, unless it gained someone's approval, nothing I did mattered. I didn't matter. I was a nobody.

I could not imagine a worse fate. In my mind, when you were a nobody, if you spoke, no one heard you; if you moved, no one saw you. It was as if you didn't exist. Nothing you did or said or wrote affected anything or anyone. I worried that if I traveled too long in my current direction, I'd wind up stranded in Nowhere Land with all the other nobodies.

Here's the strange thing about waiting tables and having no accomplishment to point to, no stage to stand on, no published book on any shelf: I still felt like somebody. No matter how little I felt there was in my life, no matter how ashamed I felt at times of my profession, no matter how long it had been since I had heard applause, I still felt like somebody. I felt like somebody when I hung around with my wife, whenever we made each other laugh, whenever she gave me her patient attention as I talked through something I was trying to understand. I felt like somebody when I was with my boys, simply walking beside them to swim lessons, putting their breakfast on the table, kissing them good night, knowing that everything I did or said mattered yet could never fully perceive why.

And I certainly felt like somebody when I plugged into that stream from which the writing flowed, when I forgot I was a waiter and a husband a father and a son and a brother and fell down into the dream of the story I was telling. I didn't feel like Bill Kenower when I plugged in, but I felt on purpose, I felt alive, I felt directed, I felt like a dog who had gotten the scent. I couldn't feel any better than that, even though I'd forgotten about Bill but remembered something else that Bill had mostly forgotten. When I went down into that dream, I wasn't so much somebody or nobody but everybody. That's how it felt first when I was writing fiction, because when I wrote fiction I had to be all the different characters, none of whom were me but all of whom I had to understand as if they were me, the same way I tried to understand my wife who wasn't me but who suffered and rejoiced as I would, the same way I had to understand my boys or coworkers or the guests whose names I didn't know. The only way to understand someone is to see yourself in them, to see where you overlap, which is always in love and fear and grief and happiness. It's not so hard; it's always there. Which is why writers and actors can seem to become other people because they weren't ever really themselves in the first place.

I learned to do it first writing fiction, but I also did it when I left the restaurant and started writing nonfiction, when there was always a character named Bill Kenower in just about every story I told. I wasn't writing about me. That was the first lesson I had to learn when I moved away from fiction. I wasn't writing about me any more than when I wrote fiction. The readers didn't care about Bill Kenower. The readers cared about themselves. What's more, I didn't know who the readers were, I didn't know if they were old or young, male or female, gay or straight, all I knew is that they *were*, and that they wanted to feel good, and that they probably didn't feel good as often as they liked, and that they always wanted to feel loved and important and on purpose. I knew that, and that was enough. If I could write with that in mind, forget Bill but remember what it is just to be human, I could tell a story for someone else so they might remember also.

It was after writing a bunch of these stories that I found myself standing on stage again. I had been asked to give a morning keynote address at a conference in Portland. I'd been out of the restaurant for a bunch of years, had given talks here and there, but this was a new conference, a new venue. I didn't know until the night before my talk that I'd be addressing six hundred people. *That's a lot of people,* I thought. That's more people than I'd ever talked to at one time.

As I began the talk, just as I was becoming lost in the stories I was telling, I noticed that standing there behind that podium, with all those eyes on me, I felt transparent. It was as if I was losing my awareness of Bill as all my attention moved to the story I was telling. In fact, I realized I couldn't *give* this talk if my attention remained on Bill. And I loved it.

One of the dreams of fame is the belief in the overwhelming validation it will provide. All the attention and approval, whether it comes through applause or book sales or retweets, will remind the artist of their value, assure them they are good enough and that they have what it takes. Even more than money, that attention can feel like the closest thing to absolute evidence that you've really *got it.* To receive that attention is to finally be free from the threat of obscurity, which is a kind of death. If you're unimportant, if you're a nobody, then it's like you don't exist, and isn't that just death in life? Isn't the artist hoping to achieve a kind of immortality from their work? I may have passed on, but my words and name will live forever!

Yet it's a backward understanding of the artist-audience relationship. When I first started doing video interviews with authors, I created a short inspirational compilation of quotes from those conversations called "The Writing Spirit." I wanted a piece that focused on the spiritual nature of writing, how work *comes* to the writer, how writing can teach who we are and how to live. The video went a bit viral, which meant it got a bunch of comments, the absolute first of which was, "I call bullshit. This has all been said before."

And I thought: That's absolutely true. Everything, really, has been said before. Every memoir ever written, for instance, is usually the same the story: *I thought I wasn't good enough, smart enough, attractive enough, and then I learned that I was.* We tell this story again and again because we need to hear it again and again. The job of the artist is to find the way of expressing these eternal ideas in a way that is unique to them, born of their unique life and experience and point of view so that audience can see the world and its true value with fresh eyes. This sharing of something eternal, whether it is love or courage or compassion or kindness, is the true immortality the artist seeks. It won't come from having our names recited when we're dead, or from having our books studied in college courses for centuries, but from seeing and sharing something that has always been.

The form of what we share isn't actually that important. Your audience will forget that form, forget most of the characters' names, most of what they did, nearly all of what they said, and they may even forget who told the story, but the audience will remember how that story left them feeling and what it helped them remember. When I think of the stories I tell in this way, it helps *me* remember who I am. If I am anything at all, it is not this body wandering around my city, nor the books with my name on it, nor my actions or deeds, but something eternal that I can recognize in myself and in others, something that as soon as I see it, I know again is love.

CHAPTER FIFTEEN

Preparing for Success

I was out of the restaurant and had started *Author* magazine and had been writing my daily blog for a couple years. I loved writing those little essays. Sometimes the ideas one sparked had me so excited that I would get up from my chair in the middle of writing and pace my room exploring the idea aloud. I was alone in my office, but I wasn't talking to myself; no, I was talking to crowds of people or small groups of people or sometimes just one very interested person. It's easier to talk when you know you're being listened to, even if the one listening is in your imagination.

The more I wrote the essays, the more time I spent imagining I was talking to people about the ideas contained in them. Once I was going for a run on a track near our house, my mind a little dulled by the repetition of going around and around and around, and soon I was picturing myself at a writers' conference talking to the crowd gathered for dinner. I'd yet to do such a thing, and I wondered what I might say if given the chance. "You're all different," I told the imaginary crowd in my running daydream. "You can't avoid it. No one's ever loved who you've loved, seen what you've seen, kissed who you've kissed, lost what you've lost. You've never happened before and you'll never happen again." *That's a good one*, I thought. Except it *was* just pretend. I hadn't actually told anyone anything. But it was a still a good one.

Then one afternoon I was going for a walk, and as usual it wasn't long before I was imagining myself talking to groups of strangers. In fact, to say I was on a walk is misleading; that would suggest I was enjoying the stream beside the path, the spring air, the faces of the strangers I passed. I was no more aware of these peripheral details than I was the world outside my window when I wrote. All my attention was in the imaginary hall where I had been asked to speak. I was crossing a little footbridge, still daydreaming about my speech, when the sound of the water running over rocks in the riverbed penetrated my awareness.

That's a beautiful sound, like nature talking. I stopped walking and stood on the bridge, listening to it. For a moment I felt self-conscious, as if the river had caught me playing pretend. I leaned on the railing and looked down at the running water. *I have to find a way to talk to people,* I thought. *I have to find out if I actually like doing it.*

I had a point. There's a difference between thinking you'd enjoy doing something and actually doing it. You find out when you do it, the same way you find out if an idea is a good idea when you take it to the blank page. The next day I began adding a line to the end of my daily blog posts about how if you liked the ideas, I was available to talk to your writing group or organization.

As is my wont, I immediately began picturing how such an experience would go. I would be invited to speak to a group of five or six writers in Seattle. I'd drive to a nearby home where I'd drink tea and talk for around forty minutes about creativity and trusting yourself, for which I'd be paid a hundred—well, fifty dollars. Fifty would be fine. I didn't care about the money. I just wanted to talk, to teach people.

A week later I got an e-mail from a reader. She absolutely wanted me to come speak to her writing organization. Fabulous, I wrote back. Who are you and where are you? She was the president of the Eastern Washington Chapter of the Society of Children's Book Writers and Illustrators (the SCBWI). They were in Spokane, a good five-hour drive from Seattle. She said she'd love to have me give a two-hour talk. She expected fifty or sixty people to attend.

This was not the plan. This was too far away, and too long a talk to too many people. I decided I'd quote her a price she couldn't possibly accept. I wrote back explaining that for this sort of thing, and considering travel time, I usually charged $500—no, $750. I said I understood if this was too high, but I was flattered for the invitation. I was a little relieved when she replied that this *was* a lot of money for her relatively small organization. She asked if I had recorded any examples of my public speaking.

As it happens, six months earlier I had been invited to be on a panel about digital publishing (I was the editor of an online magazine, remember) at a writing festival on Vashon Island, Washington. I'd also delivered a little ten-minute inspirational talk as a part of the festival's opening ceremony. Turns out that talk had been recorded, and I managed to get a copy and upload it to YouTube. I sent the link with a note about how I thought this was a pretty good example of my lectures, though in truth it remained the only one I'd ever given. A day later the reader wrote back saying that they would hold bake sales if necessary but that she definitely wanted me to come. *Crap*, I thought. *What have I done?*

I had no idea how this would go. I had a series of e-mails with Mary, the SCBWI chapter president, in which she asked me what I'd be talking about and what we would call the lecture. I had no idea. My initial plan for my talks to small writing groups in Seattle had been for people to just ask me a lot of questions. So, I came up with a title that vaguely encompassed my writing philosophy. I decided I'd break the lecture in half, with the first hour devoted to writing and the second hour to publishing.

I made a PowerPoint to serve as a kind of outline for the talk. The PowerPoint felt like a lifeline, a charted course through the unknown waters of a lecture. Here's an interesting detail about that PowerPoint. I had only one slide devoted to the second hour of the lecture, and it simply read: PUBLISHING. I never thought to add another.

However, I set to preparing what I would say for the *first* half. I loaded the PowerPoint into my computer in my office and practiced delivering the lecture to no one. Now I wasn't pretending the way I used to; now I was rehearsing, and it felt strange. I was aware that I was alone. It's one thing to practice something you've memorizing word for word; it's another to practice something that will be more or less improvised. Every time I ran through the first half of the lecture, it changed. I never said anything the same way twice. I wrote notes on index cards (again, only for the first half), hoping this would ground me to the order of my thoughts, but I kept changing what I'd say as new thoughts came to me.

I don't know how to prepare for this, I thought. *I've never done this before.* You have to prepare for things you haven't done. You have to practice and learn how to do it before you can do it. You can't just do it. But I don't know how to do it and I don't know how to prepare for it.

Meanwhile, I never practiced, outlined, or worried about the second half. One day I was in the shower and I thought, *I'll just talk about this, this, and that. That should cover it.*

That was the entire extent of my preparation for half of the talk.

The lecture was a couple months away. The first time I tried to imagine that day, tried to picture myself having a successful experience, all I saw was me alone in front of people, not saying anything, just standing there about to begin. I couldn't summon anything more reassuring than that. The idea that this talk wouldn't go well was entirely unacceptable. Two hours is a long time to be alone in front of people if things aren't going well. Yet every time I thought, *I'm going to give that talk in two months*, I'd feel the hollow dread of the inexperienced. *I can't live like this for two months*, I thought. *I can't let this talk ruin my life until it comes.*

I thought of when Jen was pregnant with Max, our first. There's a lot you can conceivably worry about when you're pregnant. Babies die and mothers die, for starters. Because Jen was the pregnant one, because she could feel Max kicking (and sometimes not kicking! *Why isn't he kicking?*), because she was the one who would actually be pushing this child out of her body and into the world, she was the one who got to worry. She'd ask me, "Do you think it's going to be okay?" And I'd reply, "I think it's going to go just fine." I knew nothing about delivering babies, but I did feel like I knew about things turning out just fine. So that was my job while she was pregnant: to remember that things turned out fine.

I decided for the upcoming talk I needed to be both a pregnant mother and a reassuring father. Every time I worried about the lecture, I'd say to myself, "I think it's going to go just fine." That would be the end of it. Until I worried again, and then I'd repeat, "I think everything is going to be just fine." This went on right up until I was sitting in my gate in SeaTac Airport waiting for my flight. Two people sat down directly behind me. I had my back to them, but they were so close that as they began talking to each other it was as if they were in my head.

"Whenever I give a talk," a woman said, "I simply follow the PowerPoint. I don't prepare every single thing I'm going to say. There's no need. I just talk about whatever's on the current slide and everything goes fine."

I didn't worry about the talk again.

Mary met me at the Spokane terminal and drove me to the venue. I had about two hours before I was to begin. I set up my PowerPoint and tested it and got some lunch. Mary asked me about what I was working on and I described my current project and told her a story about an author I'd just interviewed who'd dreamed the critical plot point for her novel. We both concurred that dreams can be very useful but aren't that reliable. We both wished we could employ our dreams like secretaries, but they seemed determined to help us on their own schedule.

People began filing in. The event was being held in a large classroom at Gonzaga University. I sat behind the professor's desk, and watched as the attendees paid for their tickets. What did they think was going to happen in this room? I wasn't entirely sure myself. Soon it was time to start, and I began by playing a short inspirational video I'd made. It was a series of some of my favorite quotes from the authors I'd interviewed. As it wound up, it occurred to me that I'd made that video in part because I hadn't been quite ready to say what I wanted to say aloud and so I'd had these authors say it for me.

Then the lights in the room went up and I began for real. At first, I talked loudly and a bit too fast. I had the sense that I needed to be just a little funnier and a little smarter and a little more interesting than I actually was, and that if I paused for even a moment, the audience would stand up as one and leave. There was a stocky, bearded man sitting dead center in the room wearing a plaid shirt. His arms were folded tightly across his chest and he had the expression of someone standing guard over a cherished idea that was under assault. I figured I'd lost him. Best not to focus on the ones who weren't with you.

My eyes drifted to the front row, where Mary was leaning forward on her desk and listening closely. I'd been more or less following what I'd planned to say, but seeing her I thought of the story of the author and her dream. It seemed like just the right thing for that moment, so I shared it and it seemed to go over well. Something in me relaxed then. It was reassuring to be able to use a story I'd only just found. I stopped trying to be smarter and funnier and more interesting than I actually was, and I started letting myself pause if I needed to think of what to say next. During one such pause my eyes swept over the audience and I noticed the bearded man was smiling and his arms were hanging by his side.

A bit later I was talking about pitching books at writers' conferences and how uncomfortable this experience can be for writers who are often introverts by nature. I said what I'd planned to say about trusting your material, but my performer's instincts didn't think it had quite landed firmly enough with the audience. *What else could I say?* I wondered. I remembered the story of the first time I'd pitched and how nervous I'd been leading up to it.

So I started telling that story. I'd always liked that story because of how absurd my fears were, and how kind the agent had been, how she couldn't have been more different from the cruel New York publishing diva I'd imagined. I'd told this story to waiters and cooks at the restaurant, to my wife, to my mom and brother and sister and my dad, and to other writers. I'd been telling it for years. Now I was telling it to this group of strangers who'd paid money to give up their Saturday afternoon, and the story was working, and right there in the middle of telling it, it hit me: I'd been preparing for this talk my entire life.

All the stories I loved to tell were preparing me. All my failures and experiments were preparing me. All my love of writing and pretend lectures were preparing me. Nothing was wasted. Nothing was make-believe. It was so simple, so obvious, so natural, it was almost disappointing.

The second half of the talk, by the way, the one I hadn't "prepared" for, went just fine, too.

A couple years later I was sitting at an awards banquet at a big writers' conference. I was a board member for this particular conference, and the board's president came up to me in the middle of the ceremony and asked if I'd be willing to go up at the end of it and help wrap it up. "Then say something inspirational to everyone," she said.

I sat eating my dinner, wondering what I would say. I tried out a couple things in my head but didn't really like them. Then I remembered. The last award was handed out and I hustled up on stage and turned to the crowd and started telling them that they were all original, and that no one had ever loved what they'd loved or lost what they'd lost and kissed or who they'd kissed, and if they didn't tell their story, no one would, so go out and tell that story.

I THINK OF moments like that and of my talk in Spokane when I look at Jack. I have no doubt that his experiences he had when he was so young, ignoring the other children and going deep into his bubble, were preparing him for something later on in life. There will come a time when all the challenges of his early life will be invaluable to him, when he will be able to employ what he learned then to surprising effect, and that what he learned will be of use not only to himself, but to others, that in his own way he will become a teacher, as absolutely everyone does when they recognize and accept what they have learned. I know all this is true now, I just don't know what the learning and teaching will look like when they meet.

The same is, of course, true for you. Prepare for your writing life by taking classes and by going to conferences and by reading books and by writing, writing, writing. But know that your life, every inch and second of it, is preparing you in ways you can't possibly perceive. Your life is the classroom that is never dismissed, and whose curriculum was conceived specifically for you.

CHAPTER SIXTEEN

Keeping Up with Yourself

I began talking about leaving the restaurant almost as soon as my wife and I learned that we'd inherited some money. Jen wanted me to leave, but she was also worried about me. "You have to do *something* for yourself first," she told me one night. "Anything. Take a class, join a group. Do something *different*."

I don't usually take advice, but I knew as soon as I heard hers that she was right. Since I'd begun writing novels, my routine had gone unchanged. I wrote first thing in the morning, did some errands, had lunch with Jen, and went to work. The only people I "shared" my work with were agents and editors. The entire publishing community seemed to exist elsewhere, on distant islands to which I sent my manuscripts and from which they were usually returned.

Meanwhile, I assiduously avoided any contact with other writers. Seen from a distance, this would have appeared to be a strange choice. I married a writer, one of my closest friends was a writer, my brother liked to write, and anytime I met anyone who showed any interest in the written word, even if it was reading suspense novels by authors I'd never heard of, I would squeeze every drop of writing and story-related conversation I could out of them. And yet at no time did I think I should try to find more writers to hang around with. It seemed like a risky proposition. My desire to compare myself was too strong, and my shame that I had not had any success was too constant. So, I largely kept myself in a writing bubble, a little cocoon where I created and sent things away, safely hidden from view until such time as I could step out proudly into the light of public opinion, fully clothed in the robes of a published author.

But having sensed Jen was right, I soon found myself flipping through a list of classes for the University of Washington's extension program. I didn't realize until I began doing so, began picturing myself in a classroom with other students, other writers, how claustrophobic my writing bubble had become. I needed the oxygen that was other people's feedback, that was hearing other people's work, that was just talking to other people about what I loved to do.

I was reminded of an experience I had a few years into my work in the restaurant. I'd begun taking aikido three times a week. Aikido's a gentle, purely defensive martial art where students are asked at all times to be aware of their balance and their breath. I had never thought about how and when I breathed until I began my training. Breathing is just what you did if you wanted to keep living. You didn't have to pay *attention* to it. But one very busy day at the restaurant, when my section was sat all at once, and I had two orders to ring-in and another to pick up in the kitchen, plus coffee I needed to pour for a six-top, I stepped into the waiter's station, my head full of all that needed doing, and just as I was about to start ringing my first order I noticed my breathing. It was so shallow, so brief, I was virtually holding my breath.

I stopped what I was doing, put down my pad, and drew in a long, deep, extended breath through my nose and then exhaled slowly out of my mouth. As soon as I did so, I could feel my chest open up, could feel the oxygen rippling through my lungs and heart, and the muscles in my back and shoulders relaxing. I did it again. I was instantly more relaxed, and my mind felt clearer, and the pressure I'd been feeling from all that needed doing was released with it. Everything still needed to be done, but there was less pressure to do it. From that moment forward, I always made sure to pause in the middle of the busiest shifts and breathe.

I signed up for advanced literary fiction. The day of the first class arrived and I joined twenty-five other students in a large room at the university. The teacher, a local novelist, began by asking each student to give a brief synopsis of their current project as well as a short writing bio. As my turn drew nearer and nearer, as I practiced what I would say in my mind, and as the prospect of actually sharing with these strangers what I was working on loomed in my imagination, my heart began beating so loudly that for a moment I literally worried that the students sitting nearby could hear it and would wonder if something was wrong with me. My turn came and I described my book, mentioned that I'd published a novel with a tiny press, and then it was on to the next student. My heartbeat returned to normal.

For the first six weeks or so I would buy a box of cookies on the way home and then eat them all with a giant glass of red wine. You would not have known looking at me with my cookies and wine that mostly all I'd done was sit in a classroom and make the occasional comment about other students' projects (given the size of the class, in the first semester I only shared two chapters of my book). It was as if I'd spent the entire two hours bracing myself for a shock, for a trauma that never came. If you had asked, I would not have been able to tell you *exactly* what that trauma would be, though it probably would have had something to do with people reading my stuff and not liking it.

Which happened, of course. Once it was my turn to share, some people liked the pages and some people not so much. I didn't enjoy having anyone say, "I don't get it," or, "I felt the middle dragged a little," but it wasn't traumatic. In fact, it wasn't even unfamiliar. It wasn't just that I'd survived the experience again and again of having my work rejected by agents and editors, it was that I'd lived through the very common, daily experience of telling someone a joke, or sharing an idea with someone, sometimes someone very close to me, and that person not laughing at the joke or understanding the idea. I'd known this experience my whole life, the inevitable consequence of being with people who aren't me, who don't think exactly like me or believe exactly what I believe. In the end, being critiqued was not so very different from having a conversation, except that people tell you what they're thinking of what you've said.

I stopped buying the cookies, and my glass of wine got smaller. One night while driving home from the class I recalled a time not long after I first arrived in Seattle. I was lying on Jen's couch one afternoon while she ironed a blouse and told me about a class she was taking. Los Angeles was 1,200 miles away. At that moment, I had no project to work on, no career goals, no plans. In fact, except for Jen, I didn't know anyone in Seattle, and I was very happy. I was happy just to be with her. *Relax, Bill*, I thought. *It's okay to relax. It's okay not to pursue something. It's okay just to be here. Start over.*

When I began that first novel, I put myself into a bubble. I needed that bubble. I needed to do something without *immediately* trying to get it out into the world. I needed to just create, to stop thinking about success and simply be with this woman I loved and work a job and write something. I was comfortable for the first time in many years. I hadn't been comfortable trying to be a screenwriter and racing around Los Angeles in search of movie-writing fame. There'd been no rest for me there, no breathing, just running and running and running.

Fifteen years is a long time to be in a bubble. Even when I sent my work out, when I went to writers' conferences, I still felt as though I was in the safety of that cocoon because I was anonymous. None of the agents or editors that rejected my stuff knew me, they'd never met me, there was nothing personal about it; it was just a business transaction. Even when I did meet the agents at conferences, all our future correspondences happened via mail and, eventually, e-mail. I did not understand until I took that class that the bubble had actually become *un*comfortable, that I was suffocating in it.

You may have heard that it's good to "get out of your comfort zone." I think this popular advice misunderstands comfort zones. I don't like being uncomfortable—ever. In fact, writing itself is a search for the comfort of an effortless way forward. The only way I know I'm writing the story I want to write in the way I want to write it is by paying attention to the difference between the effort required to force a story in a direction, force a character to do something they wouldn't do, force a word into a sentence, and the effortlessness of finding the story's true path, of letting the characters do what they're meant to do, of finding the word that drops in like the right piece in a jigsaw puzzle. Effort and effortlessness are the guiding experiences of creativity and of life itself. Paying attention to effort and effortlessness, caring about the difference between one and the other, is the only way I *know* which way to go. There is no formula. There is no plan anyone else can lay down for me. Only I can possibly write my story and lead my life, and the only way to know if I'm writing my story and leading my life instead of someone else's is to find the comfort of the effortless path.

But if it's a path I'm following, which every story is, which every life is, then it will lead me somewhere. And if it leads me somewhere, if I'm following it and traveling, then where I go will be different from where I was. The path is *never* a circle. Like a sentence, whose each word is laid down like a paving stone across the blank page to form a completed gesture of thought, the path, which is life's ceaseless creative impulse, is evolutionary. Just as your story changes with every single sentence, so too you and your life, which are inseparable, change with every single day, whether you want that day to change you and your life or not.

This is why your job is not to get out of your comfort zone but to keep *up* with it. It moves as you evolve. That said, like a lot of artists, now that I've found the subject matter that interests me most, and now that I've found how I'm most interested in exploring that subject, it might appear from a certain distance that my comfort zone is quite stationary. For instance, since I started *Author*, I have written well over one thousand essays about the relationship between the books we write and the life we lead. But I did not write the same essay a thousand times. I could only write if I was interested and I could only be interested if I was discovering something. And so, each essay looked at that relationship from a different angle or vantage. Often, what I discovered writing one essay opened the door to the next.

Once you've found your subject matter, the movement you experience is often slight, though it is movement nonetheless. Sometimes, however, it is not so slight. A few years ago, I was speaking in Oregon about *Fearless Writing*. I'd given many such talks before, especially after publishing that book. I loved talking about *Fearless Writing*, about the challenge of forgetting to care what people think about our stuff, and about the freedom it allows, about how doing so drops everyone into the creative flow they are always seeking.

Yet in the middle of this talk, which was going just fine, I realized I was feeling a little bored with it. I could have kept going anyway. Just as an actor must find his interest in the same role he plays night after night, I knew how to find my interest in the same stories I'd told many times before. But I was not an actor and I was not playing a role and I did not have a script to follow. I thought about the talks I'd given to Rotary Clubs, how some were about being "The Author of Your Life" and some were about how "No One Is Broken." Though one focused on writing and the other on raising a son on the spectrum, they were not so very different in their trajectory.

So, I started talking about Jack and about the challenge of raising a kid like him if you believed in broken people, and about how much time I spent wondering if I *had what it took*. I felt the difference in me immediately, the exhalation of thought as my mind moved to that new, fertile terrain. I have no idea if the audience noticed a difference. If I had to guess, I would venture they didn't. But I could feel that I was onto something, and that something became this book.

However, we are often advised to get *out* of our comfort zone because, if you are like me, there is the temptation to believe that life would be simpler, would be easier, if that comfort zone never moved. Oh, if only what pleased me yesterday would please me today, if I wasn't always having to *find* it and keep up with it. What a lot of work. This desire for a stationary comfort zone is a reflection of a truth about where comfort and creativity and inspiration are always found. They are always found in exactly the same spot, a place where I can never spend enough time but which I manage to regularly avoid nonetheless. That place is the present moment.

I cannot write and be regretting the past or worrying about the future. Nor can I give a talk if I'm thinking about tomorrow's breakfast or what I talked to my wife about that morning. All creation happens in the present moment. The effortlessness I feel when in the creative flow is as much an expression of being in the present moment as it is laying my attention on the story that interests me most. It's just that *when* I'm present, when I'm not worrying whether the story I'm writing will be published or what my agent will think of it, it's easier to find the story I most want to tell and the way I want to tell it. The present moment is where everything is. It's where *I* am. There's no other place to actually be. No matter how much teleportation I attempt, I can't actually project myself into the future nor fly back into the past. I'm always right here in the right now.

> *All creation happens in the present moment.*

That's a very comfortable place to be if you can accept it. If I don't accept where I am, I *will* be uncomfortable. Accepting where I am does not mean I will be there forever. If I have not published a book and I want to publish a book, accepting where I am does not mean I will *never* publish a book. If I want to publish a book, I must accept that I have not so that I can learn how to. It's like using a GPS to get to a destination. When I use my GPS, the first thing I do is tell it where I want to go. The *next* thing I do is tell it where I am. If I don't tell the GPS where I am it can't give me directions to where I want to go. For the GPS to help me, where I am is as important as where I want to go. If I lie to it, if I tell it I'm much closer to my destination than I actually am, it will give me the wrong directions and I'll be lost. I have often given my inner GPS many inaccurate starting positions. I always think I'm closer to my destination than I actually am. I always just want to *be there*.

Except in truth the only place I ever want to be is the here and now. Yes, I want to publish more books and teach more workshops and buy a new car and probably buy a new house. Yes, I want all those things. But the route to all those destinations can always be found in the present moment, and the instant I drop in to where I actually am, the moment I stop judging where I am and accept it, be present in it, I am comfortable and I am where I want to be. As soon as I drop in to it, I think, *This is interesting*. As soon as I think something is interesting, I want to know more about it. Now I'm curious, now I'm following something, now I'm moving, and now I'm growing—but I'm still comfortable, still me, still where I want to be even as I'm headed somewhere new.

CHAPTER SEVENTEEN

Writing as Kindness

I was raised perfectly agnostic. My parents both grew up attending church in Kansas City, and my father, as I have mentioned, got a degree from Harvard Divinity School with the idea of becoming a Unitarian minister. For a time, they were regular attendees at a Congregational church in my hometown of Providence. Someone even once referred to them as "pillars of the church."

However, by the time I came along, their time spending Sunday mornings in a pew listening to sermons and singing hymns was over. Neither ever explained how this shift occurred, but I know the decision was made without animosity. Both, I believe, had fond memories of going to church, of the warm community, and the act of gathering together to think about something bigger than jobs and money and mere survival. This meant no one in my house was criticizing religion and no one was telling me I needed to be religious. Whether

I ever went to church would be up to me the same as whether I played the drums or went to college.

Not being a joiner by nature, I remained nonaffiliated in my beliefs, but I would find myself thinking about Jesus from time to time, and about the nature of his teachings—of which, in truth, I had only a cursory knowledge. No matter. One day when I was twenty-two, I was in the shower, where I did some of my very best thinking. I found myself wondering about turning the other cheek, and about people without sin throwing stones, and loving your enemy as your brother. *He's talking about always being kind to everybody no matter what,* I thought.

I had an image of a group of people at a card table, all of them holding their hands close to their chest, glancing from their competitors' eyes to the pile of coins in the center of the table. *It's as if we should all put our cards down,* I thought. Except in this game, the game of life itself, someone has to put his down first, before the others. Who would do that? You lose the game then if no one else does it. You're just the sucker who dropped his guard, who gave away his hand, who said, "I'm not playing anymore," and now the treasure will go to those still playing that game, the game of getting what you want.

I knew all about *that* game. I knew all about wanting girls and success and attention and approval and money. Some days, it felt as if I spent most of my time just wanting, wanting, wanting. I never intended to be unkind, but true kindness, kindness that asks for nothing in return, seemed risky. I feared living in a world where all those things I wanted never came to me. Maybe it's best to just look out for Number One.

I had already begun working full-time as a waiter and bartender while my brother and I performed our show around Providence. I was a good waiter insofar as I was very efficient. I could handle lots of tables at once without losing my cool. But it was very stressful. I didn't want to disappoint people, to have them waiting and waiting for their meals, or for them to get the wrong meal. This rarely happened, but the threat that it might hung over every shift I worked. I often had horrible dreams about waiting tables, where I had to serve an entire restaurant and I couldn't get the coffeemaker to work, or I couldn't ring in a single order, and still the people kept coming in and sitting there with no food, staring and staring and staring at me.

The problem with waiting tables, I thought, was the people. Not all the people, just the few troublesome ones. We called those people the "Customers from Hell." I learned to spot them right away. I could tell by the look in their eyes that they were certain they were going to be disappointed, that I would fail them somehow, that they wouldn't get what *they* wanted. Oh, I hated them sometimes, especially when I was young. I hated how they had to micromanage everything, how impatient they were to have their water refilled, how irate they'd become if their burger was a little overcooked. They were miserable people spreading their misery like a virus. I wanted to punish them. They didn't *deserve* to get what they wanted.

My father was sort of one these customers. We'd go out for lunch and he'd quickly become impatient with the server, tapping his empty water glass, looking around as soon as he'd put down his menu. Having been a server for a little, I realized his mistake. "The trick to getting good service," I told him, "is to be nice to the servers."

"What? I have to be nice to *them*? It's their job to be nice to *me*."

"I know," I said. "But they're just people. And when I'm waiting tables, if I have an extra moment, whose table am I going to visit? I'm going to visit the nice person, I'm going to go be nice to the one who's nice to me."

"That's backward. That's not how it should work."

We eventually agreed that when we ate out, I would be the one who talked to the servers. A few years later, I was working in a steakhouse in Seattle. The place I'd worked in Providence was a barbeque joint, where I made my money by serving dozens of tables in a single shift. In the steakhouse, I made twice as much money waiting on a third of the number of people. That the diners were spending so much money affected me. I wasn't impolite to the people I served in the barbeque place, but at the steakhouse, I didn't feel I could get away with the sum of my waiter-customer exchange being "What do you want?" and "Here you go." I needed to be truly polite, to listen, to be friendly no matter how busy I was or what mood I was in or whether my diners were Customers from Hell.

Once I decided I needed to be friendly no matter what, I experienced the customers being noticeably less hellish. If someone sat down and I sensed impatience and doubt in them, I would do all I could in everything I said, in every order I took and delivered, even in my silence as they discussed among themselves which appetizer to order, to make sure they knew that everything was going to be okay. That's it. That's all they wanted to know, I realized, that everything was going to be okay. They'd get what they wanted; they didn't need to worry. There are people, and I've been one of them, who believe they absolutely must worry, as if it's a kind of spell they cast against potential calamity.

I liked reassuring the diners in this way not because it meant I got better tips—which I did—and not because the more impatient and insecure the customer, the more likely they were to shake my hand like we were fast friends as they said goodbye—which they also did—but because of how good I felt the instant I chose to be friendly no matter what and to remind someone that everything was going to be okay. I couldn't remind someone else that everything was going to be okay unless I remembered it first myself. I had to find within me what I was offering to them. Just like every customer I served, I never wanted to worry and I always wanted to get what I wanted and I always wanted to be okay.

For the twenty years I waited tables, getting what I wanted was frequently on my mind. What I *wanted* was a publishing contract, acceptance, approval, recognition, success. I wanted the books I wrote to give me all of that. Once I got what I wanted, then I'd *know* that everything was okay because I'd know *I* was okay. I'd done it. I would no longer have to doubt myself. Yet I sent the books out and got nothing in return. Or so I believed. You always get something; you just may not like it or understand what it is.

When I wrote my first little essay for *Author* magazine, I

asked myself a question I had not asked myself in all the years I'd written novels: "What's the best thing I could say to my readers?" The answer was easy: *Fear not. Everything is going to be okay.* When I wrote that essay, I wasn't thinking about what that essay would give me. Partly, this was because I'd played a little trick on myself. Since I had decided that what I wanted could only come via a book contract, I didn't expect the essay to bring me what I wanted. So, with success off the table, I thought instead of what I could give my readers. I saw the piece I was writing as a gift I was giving.

Except just like those customers I had to reassure, I could not give to my readers what I did not already have myself. The gift I wanted to give had to come to me first. If I wanted to write about being fearless, I had to find fearlessness in myself first; if I wanted to write about how everything was okay, I had to find that font of unconditional well-being in me first. In this way, my choice to view writing as giving something to someone else gave me what I wanted immediately. No, not a publishing contract, but the feeling of fearlessness and of being okay. That, after all, is what I thought the publishing contract would ultimately provide—security and confidence.

Eventually, writing all those little essays did bring me a publishing contract. It took a while, but when it came, I understood the connection between the contract and that very first essay. I thought of that first contract when I was buying some bagels one morning. It was busy, and the woman in front of me in line was having a hard time deciding what to buy, asking the fellow serving her which bagels were hottest, and why were the bialy bagels more expensive, and is their cream cheese fresh, and would he slice the bagels for her, and could she switch the pumpernickel for a wheat—no, how about a sesame—or no, how about an onion? On and on it went, and in the middle of it, the young man helping her glanced up, and as our eyes met, I smiled and gave him my best commiserative former-waiter shrug. That's all. Just a little something to let him know that I thought he was doing a good job handling a difficult customer.

When my turn came, I ordered my usual baker's dozen, and as he handed me my bag, he said, "There's a little something in there for how long you had to wait." When I got home, I counted and he'd given me an extra three bagels. To be clear, I'd waited far longer before at the same bakery. I also doubted he gave three extra bagels to everyone waiting behind me. The bagels, it seemed to me, were his way of saying thank you for a simple, compassionate gesture, a gesture for which I expected absolutely nothing in return. I can never be reminded often enough that kindness is its own reward for which, ironically, we are often rewarded.

The only real difference between the bagels and a publishing contract is the speed with which the physical reward came. Once the publishing contract came, it was certainly nice, but it wasn't the life-changing event I had expected. My experience of writing the essays upon which the book was based was always the same. I'd find something about my life, some experience I'd had that, when viewed a certain way, made it seem as if everything is *not* okay. Maybe I'd lost something or felt criticized or failed or was lonely and scared. There've been lots and lots of times in my life where everything did not seem okay at all. Then I'd turn that event in my mind until I saw it differently, saw it as necessary or inevitable or just or helpful or funny. When I got to the end of the essay and I was satisfied that I'd seen the experience differently, I always felt better immediately. I felt better not because I'd accomplished anything—though in a way I had; I had accomplished successfully completing an essay. No, I felt better because I had, in writing the piece, brought my*self* to a place within me where I remembered that I was okay and everything was okay. In that moment, I had already arrived where I wanted to be.

Early on, when I was writing one of these essays five days a week, before I knew if anyone was reading them, or enjoying reading them, or caring that they'd read them, I'd always push back from the desk and think, *Well, I have no idea what's going to happen now, but I feel better, so that's a win.* Writing yourself to a place where you feel better five times a week is a fantastic practice. The more I did this, the more often I led myself to this better-feeling place, the more that destination *became* my true goal.

It was a strange goal. There was a little gremlin in my mind who would often ask, "Yeah, but what about money? What about acclaim? What about *success*?"

"I know," I'd say. "I still want those things—I think. But the problem is once I feel better I don't find myself itching for all those other things. They don't seem so important. Am I losing my edge?" I'd ask him. "Am I losing my ambition?"

"Yes," he'd reply. "You definitely are. Get hungry, buddy. Where's the yearning? Where's the drive? I think you're screwed."

It went on like this for a while. The gremlin was looking out for Number One. I'd lowered my cards, you see. I was sort of giving what I had away. Not just because I wasn't yet getting paid much for what I was doing, but because I already felt satisfied and so I didn't want anything in return. So, I kept on writing in this way, and the gremlin kept nagging me. It was uncomfortable, and I'd feel low sometimes, believing I was just drifting, wasn't heading anywhere, wasn't *striving*.

I was still flesh and blood, after all. I still needed money, and wanted enough of it to live comfortably. I still wanted *things*. Things are fun. And publishing a book is fun. Writing the book is the best part, but publishing it is great, too. I love working with a publisher, the collaboration of it, and I love that once it's published *anyone* can just pick it up and have the experience of reading it, that I don't need to *do* anything for that to happen. But all the things I can buy and all the contracts and e-mails from readers cannot replace the satisfaction I feel the instant I am led by what I am writing to where I want to be.

It doesn't matter what you write, by the way. I write these inspirational stories about my life, but everyone is led by what they write to where they want to be. If you love fantasy literature, then within you is a place where you go when you read fantasy and when you write it. It's the same place, really. You know it well. Once you've spent a lot of time there, you can easily talk to other people who love fantasy literature. They have a place within themselves where they go that loves fantasy, too. The fantasy stories you write and sell will be an act of kindness because even though you will be paid for these stories—and you will be, if you aren't already—you are still giving the story away. You are saying to your reader, "Here. I've written this. It's great. Writing it made me so happy. Now it's yours. It's all yours. Do with it what you want. Dream from it, live in it, picture the characters however you want. It's yours, it's yours, it's yours. I wanted you to have it."

It's an act of kindness because in the act of writing it you weren't thinking about money, or rewards, or fame. Not *while* you were writing it. While you were writing it, all you were thinking about was the story and how much you loved it and how cool it was and how you wanted to find out how it really ended. *That's* what you were thinking about. That's all you *can* think about. You can't think about acclaim and fame and money while you're writing a story. The moment you do, you're not writing a story anymore. Whether you're aware of it or not, while you're writing, you're expecting nothing in return. While you're writing, the writing is its own reward.

It has always been so. You wouldn't be writing if it wasn't so. I've never met a successful writer who began writing with the express purpose of making a lot of money. Every single one of those writers, myself certainly included, began writing because the writing was its own immediate reward. Then these writers became adults, if they weren't already, and they had to figure out how writing could also bring them the things adults need to survive, which complicated the process for some (like me) and not for others. Either way, the writing remains an act of kindness, of loving something—a story—unconditionally.

The gremlin, by the way, still talks to me from time to time. There's just no convincing him that kindness alone will bring us all that we want. He believes it must be more complicated than that. There *must* be hard work involved; there must be an obstacle to overcome. That poor gremlin was born in and has lived forever in hell, an unfriendly place where no two people share anything but misery and no one has what they want—yet they want and want and want just the same. Hell is eternal wanting, eternal waiting, endless desire without satisfaction, life as we wanted it like a picture in a magazine of people who look more or less like me but must be different somehow for they are happy.

The gremlin's real problem is that he's impatient. Writing requires waiting. Sometimes what I want—the idea, the scene, the sentence, the word—comes to me quickly and fluidly as water from a tap. Other times, I have to wait. I can *feel* what I want, I'm hovering around it, but the form has not come. That doesn't mean I don't *have* it. I'm sitting in it. Just like the fantasy writer who must sit in the world of fantasy literature, sit in what is so lovely about it, I must always sit in whatever I'm writing about, rest in it as a felt experience of life before I can receive the words I need to give it a shape I can share with other people. Where I sit is the Garden of Creation. It's a place where there is no good or bad, there is no right or wrong, just the story I want to tell and what belongs in it and what does not. What a lovely place, what a happy place, a place for everyone always. Go there and you have what you want instantly, and in so doing can happily find a way to give it to others.

CHAPTER EIGHTEEN

Writing as a Relationship

I discovered shortly after I began interviewing authors that I could perform a kind of parlor trick. I could guess, with about 90 percent accuracy, whether a writer outlined a little, a lot, or not at all. No one was this truer for than the crime writer James Lee Burke, whom I interviewed in 2018. I was familiar with his name and his reputation but not his work. However, I was certain after reading one page of his novel *Robicheaux* that this man did not outline. That is not to say it lacked focus; quite the opposite. But I sensed something improvisational about his language, and, sure enough, he confirmed that he never knew after that first paragraph what was going to happen in his novels. He was an absolutely true "pantser," discovering the story as he wrote it.

We found ourselves in a discussion about the mysterious nature of creativity, and he mentioned how William Faulkner, on his deathbed, said, "If I hadn't written my stories, some other hand would have." Burke felt much the same way about his novels.

"Every artist knows this," he said. "Whatever the artist's faith or lack of faith, he must concede this: It comes from somewhere else. The day the artist takes credit for it is the day that artist will lose it."

I agree with Burke completely except for the losing it part—though I know experientially that taking full credit for whatever I've written closes the door to where the ideas come from until such time as I admit the truth of it, at which point the door always opens again.

And the truth of it is this: Something else provides the ideas and the inspiration; I translate them.

In this way, I have come to view writing as a relationship. To describe it in any other way would be inaccurate. I had always been a little shy about this reality. I would never be able to prove this relationship, and I was afraid of sounding grandiose if I talked about writing in these terms. But to say "I came up with an idea" was never true. Ideas come to me. At best, I allow them in, accept and explore them. But I don't make them. I don't know how.

This relationship in which every creative person is engaged is another reason we often feel like we don't have what it takes. Viewed a certain way, I don't have *everything* it takes to write anything. I simply can't do this alone. I've tried, and it was miserable. I was just typing, feeling as if I had forgotten how to write. It's a very dead feeling, writing a story as a zombie might, with flesh and bone and a mind but no actual life.

You will have to decide for yourself what to call that which

you are relating to when you write. The word doesn't matter,
I don't think. What does matter is that you acknowledge
you're in a relationship and that you cannot and never have
been able to do this alone. If you're like me, once you accept
this, writing can get much easier.

I've noticed my writing relationship is very much like the
relationships I have with actual live human beings. Every relationship I've ever been in, whether with a girlfriend when I
was young or with my wife for the past thirty years, whether
with my sons or my family or friends or a stranger I meet at
the park—every one of these relationships goes better the less
I require of that other person. The less I need the other person
to be happy for me to be happy, or the less I need the other
person to say a certain thing or do a certain thing for me to
feel happy or loved or acceptable, the easier it is to relate to
that person.

That sounds simple enough stated this way, but it's a bit
more complicated in practice. So much in life requires another person's willing participation, from making love to having a conversation to publishing a book. It can be quite
frustrating when you feel like you know what you want but
you just can't figure out how to get the other people required
to come along and join in. Everyone's will is as free as mine.
When Jack was three, he plopped himself down in front of his
plastic Winnie-the-Pooh drum set and composed a song
whose only lyrics were:

You have to get along
But you gotta have free

Hearing this, I thought, *Well, there's the whole human condition right there.* We all have to get along with others. We have to get along when we got to school, if we have a job, if we want a girlfriend or a boyfriend. We stop at red lights, we're quiet in libraries, and we put our dogs on leashes. All of this is getting along. And aren't we getting along when we publish a book? Aren't we looking for editors and readers who want what we want, hoping the story we told can become a part of the great cooperative, societal conversation?

But you also have to have free. You've got to live your life. Not mine, not Shakespeare's, not Joyce Carol Oates's, but yours. If you're not living your unique, authentic life, then what's the point? How is that even living? Sometimes getting along and being free can seem in conflict. What if I don't want to go to school or watch that show or do this work? Everyone else is running around wanting what they want, and sometimes those people say, "You need to vote this way or write this way or drive this way or sing this way to be happy or to be a good person or to be accepted into the tribe of man."

Jack saw this complication at an early age and decided getting along wasn't worth the risk. So, in he went, in where no one could tell him what to do—not teachers or his parents or other children. He explained as much to me years later when he had decided that he wanted a girlfriend and a job and a life that looked more or less like everyone else's. "I just didn't want other people to influence me," he explained. "I just wanted to be left alone."

Oh, did I understand this. Part of the reason writing so appealed to me was that I felt like I had found something that didn't require anyone else. Yes, there was the publishing thing, and that did not go so well for a while. But the *actual* writing, that I could do alone, couldn't I? I'm the only one in the room, aren't I? Yes, I am, and thank God for that. Now I can finally pay attention to what I would like to say instead of worrying about what other people wanted me to say. Now I don't have to bother trying to figure out how to get along. Now I can be free.

Until, that is, I sat there alone at my desk, with no idea in my heart, and tried to write anyway. Not only did I feel like an impotent Doctor Frankenstein, trying to bring to life what was utterly and stubbornly dead, but I felt trapped, sealed alone in a car whose engine couldn't run. It ran yesterday but not today. I turned the key, I pressed the pedals, but nothing. And all around me people were driving and driving and driving. *What's wrong with me?* I wondered. I asked the question, but I dreaded the answer. Whatever it was, I was certain it couldn't be fixed.

As Jack decided he wanted to rejoin society, we spent more and more time running errands together. Whereas he once wanted to stay in all the time, now if he heard me grabbing my keys, he was up and out of his room and wanting to come along. He still had a habit, however, of talking to himself in public, a habit that had begun in his early childhood when he spent all his time in his cocoon. He had been doing it for so long, he usually didn't even notice when he was. Before he became interested in coming out of his shell, if we were out and about and he was talking to himself and I pointed it out, he'd get angry and tell me to mind my own business. Now he allowed me to mention it, hoping it would help him break the habit.

We were at Costco one day, rolling along through the aisles, when I heard the familiar sound of his muttering beside me. I tapped him on the arm. "You're doing it."

He sighed and his shoulders sagged. "You know what it is, Dad? I just get bored."

I was once again amazed how similar he and I were. I could get bored, bored, bored in the middle of a conversation or just about anything, really. I didn't like being bored, and so I'd learned to retreat into my mind, where I could pursue something silently that *was* interesting to me. It's a problematic habit, particularly in a marriage, one I had been gradually breaking.

"I get it," I said. "It's just a matter of patience. If you just give other people a little time, just wait a moment, you usually learn what they're getting to. Just give them a little time and it can get interesting."

I'd learned this firsthand when I interviewed authors. I don't write questions down ahead of time. I did at first, but those questions were based on who I thought the writer was having read their work, but then I'd meet them and I'd learn so much about them just by the way they'd say "Hello," that the questions were no longer useful. So, instead of using prepared questions, I'd listen. I'd listen to the author, of course, but I'd simultaneously listen to myself, listen for what was interesting to me about what they were saying. To do this, I had to surrender any notions of what I thought we *should* be talking about, or even what I thought I was interested in. I had to give up control. In the best conversations, the ideas we were exploring, the story we were telling, belonged to both of us. Neither of us could fully claim it for ourselves.

I had a chance to interview Kami Garcia and Margaret Stohl after they published their breakout YA novel, *Beautiful Creatures*. I was interested in their writing process since, unlike screenwriters, novelists rarely work in pairs. Each would write a chapter and then send it to the other, who would then go through and make changes and then send it back to the other and so on and so on. At one point, Kami phoned Margaret to tell her she just *had* to cut a certain paragraph. Kami was prepared for a fight with her partner, whom she was certain would want to defend her work. "Go ahead and cut it," Margaret said. "You wrote it."

Theirs was a particularly egoless process, as neither could ever take full credit for anything. Apparently, they couldn't even remember what they wrote. I was reminded of this when I published one of my early books. The editor sent back the manuscript in a Word document with all her many line edits highlighted in that application's handy Track Changes feature. Every single word, comma, or hyphen she'd changed was highlighted and underlined. Since I'd written the thing, I decided I should go through the entire book, change by change, to make sure I agreed with her suggestions. This I did for about five pages before I got sick of it.

Instead, I turned the Track Changes feature off. This hid, or unhighlighted, her edits. I then read it without knowing what she had changed, and if I came across something I didn't like, or wasn't quite what I meant, I'd rewrite it. Mostly, I was fine with the changes, even though I wasn't certain which sentences were *all mine*, and which she had altered. I had thought I needed to go through the manuscript edit by edit so I could know the book was mine, that by clicking *Accept* on every "and" or "but" or "however" she'd added or deleted I'd feel like I'd actually written those altered sentences. I was the author, after all. Didn't I care about all those changes? Not really. As long as I liked what I read, I was fine with putting my name to it.

The editor also dotted each chapter with questions: *What did you mean about there being no coincidence? What are you referring to here when you refer to painful history? Did you mean to contradict yourself in these two paragraphs?* Each question pointed out where my writing was a little unclear, asking me to go back in and either add a word or two, or, in a few cases, reimagine what I meant to say. I may have written the answers to her questions myself, but would I have found that new stuff without her help? Her questions were the inspiration, the creative catalyst for my new thought.

The writer-editor partnership is an extension of the author's personal, ongoing creative process. Both require surrender. With an editor, I must surrender my manuscript to another person's aesthetic and critical attention. After all, every word on that page was a choice I made. Some of the choices I made quickly and some I thought about for quite a while. At the time I made them, I believed they were the best choice; I wouldn't have made them otherwise. Then along comes the editor, and she says, "Let's make some different choices here and there." Do I get a little angry when I first see the marked-up manuscript lacerated with red lines? Why, yes, I do. For a moment, my editor is my adversary in a war of choices. Remember, I'm a little competitive. How easy it is to see her changes as my choice having lost and hers having won. How easy to forget we are on the same team, with the same goal. We are working together to create something entertaining and inspiring to share with other people. This is getting along.

It's also having free. That first time I read a chapter without the changes highlighted, I felt relieved. How nice to remember that I am more than my choices or my ideas. I once got into an argument with an old friend, in the middle of which he said, "If you don't like my ideas, you don't like me. I *am* my ideas!" It was the first time I'd heard this belief stated so baldly. How absurd. Ideas are just thoughts, and thoughts can change. My ideas have changed and changed and changed over my life, and yet I remain essentially the same person, the one in search of ideas that best suit me. I have sought ideas that align with who I am, but I can still discard those ideas. They're like clothing. If they don't fit, or I don't like how I look in them anymore, they have to go. I am bigger than a single idea, than a single point of view, than a single book. Nothing I write will ever be as complete as I have always been.

Then there is the surrender necessary just to write. Every time I sit down at my desk, I must surrender to the present moment. It was the memoirist and poet Sheila Bender who pointed out to me that when we write stories about our own life, about our past, we are in actuality writing about the present. How I write about seeing my wife for the first time or what it was like to catch a pass or get a rejection letter changes with the calendar. How I describe those things today may not be the same as how I describe them in a year or month. The present moment is always wholly original. It's also beyond my control. I can control what I choose to remember, and I can control what I choose to dream about, how I picture the future. The present moment, what actually *is*, cannot be controlled. It can only be joined and collaborated with.

There is no surrender in life more important than this one, the surrender to the reality that is the present moment. When people ask where ideas come from—that's the real answer. If I want those ideas, if I want that inspiration, then I have to be where the ideas are. I have spent a lot of time mentally elsewhere, reliving the past or anticipating the future, trying to make life what I want it to be, trying to be happy. When I sit down to write, I have to surrender that search. I am not giving up when I do so, though I have from time to time believed I was. Rather, I am accepting my role in the creative process that is writing and is life. I can either join and collaborate with reality, with life, or fight against it.

Surrender can mean different things to us. It will always mean the end of the fight, but I must decide if ending the fight means victory or loss. In a war, the one who surrenders has lost, has given up their idea of how things should be. I cannot fight with reality; it is impervious to my demands or assaults. It is also without judgment on me. I *can* take credit for what I've written, and I have. While this closes the door to new ideas, for in taking credit I have decided I can and will go it alone, the source of those ideas does not hold a grudge. As soon as I am ready to resume the relationship, as soon as I open that door again, I am instantly and completely forgiven.

CHAPTER NINETEEN

No Drama

I had reached my lowest moment. My fourth novel had just been rejected, I was about to turn forty, and I was still waiting tables. I came home from work one night, my mind roiling with frustration. My wife and kids were asleep, but I couldn't rest. I sat in my living room, staring at my life, at all I hadn't accomplished, filled with shame and confusion, and for the first—and only—time in my life I thought, *Death would be better than how I feel right now.*

That got my attention. I didn't want to die, but I felt as if I had wandered to the edge of a cliff from which I might fall accidentally. I knew then I had to do something differently. I didn't know what that would be, but I accepted then that something I was doing simply wasn't working for me.

The next night, in middle of my shift, as I was delivering the check to a chatty couple, the man reached for the bill and said, "Thank you. That was wonderful." I bowed slightly, said,

"My pleasure," and stepped away to greet a table of four who'd just been seated. Yet I was aware that something about the man's simple, appreciative statement stayed with me. Some part of my mind was still hanging on to it, feeding off of it, wringing it as if it was a damp rag and I was dying of thirst.

I stood for a moment in my section, between tables, and all at once, I saw it: I'd been living my whole life for other people's recognition and approval. I couldn't remember a time when that wasn't the single, sustaining goal in my life, the thing I believed I needed to be happy. And the truth was, I'd gotten it. I may not have published a novel, but all my life I'd been recognized for my athletic ability, my artistic talent, my intelligence, my sense of humor, my looks. Why, I even had a job where my very income seemed based on whether people recognized and appreciated my service. I'd been recognized and recognized and recognized, and yet I still wasn't happy.

The next day I decided I simply had to stop caring what people thought about me, accept that it was an empty, addictive motivator. I knew it would take practice, that I simply couldn't turn a switch and stop caring, but that was okay; if there's one thing I knew how to do, it was practice. Yet that evening, as I sat again in my living room contemplating this practice, picturing life without caring what people thought about me, I saw one potential problem: Where's the fun?

For all the pain and emptiness my search for approval had brought me, it gave my life structure, gave it a destination where there'd be applause and laughter and people saying nice things about me. What would get me up in the morning without that? I felt a bit like a soldier who'd been decommissioned, his services no longer necessary, for the enemies had all surrendered.

A few months later I was feeling a bit low and complaining to my wife. She'd been listening to me complain plenty, and on this evening, she had an idea. "Will you just listen to this teacher I found recently? She's awesome and I think it would be helpful."

I said I didn't want to listen to any damn teacher, and besides, I needed to go to work soon.

"Please," she said. "There's this clip that's only fifteen minutes. It's great and she's really funny. Please, just listen. What's the harm?"

I said fine. Just play it. This way I could say I'd listened and maybe she'd quit trying to help me.

Jen was right. The teacher was quite funny. I trusted funny. Also, she started talking about how everyone is creative and how we're always creating things whether we like it or not. I liked this, and I thought it was absolutely true. Then she started talking about happiness. She said happiness was our natural state of being, that we are meant to be happy, that this is the whole point of being alive.

She was not the first teacher, or first person for that matter, to say this. I'd heard it plenty before, but on this evening, after what I'd been through recently, I thought, *That is the exact opposite of how I've been living. I've seen happiness as something you assemble from achievement and success. I'll bet she's right.*

I thought about happiness as I drove to work that night. I

thought first about all the things that had happened in my life that seemed to have *made* me happy: the first time I'd met Jen, winning a race, getting a good review for the show I did with my brother, getting a call from an agent. Thinking about those things, I could feel the lightness and relief that came when life seemed to be working out for me, when I believed everything was going to be okay.

Then I thought about other things that made me happy. I thought how listening to music or telling jokes or watching a good show could make me happy. I could think about the movies I've loved, and the friends I've had, and the songs that had lifted me when I was down, and even though I was just driving in my car, I could still feel that joy, that alive hum within me they'd brought, even though I wasn't listening or talking or watching anything.

By then I was downtown and looking for a place to park. I found a spot, turned off the car, grabbed my work bag, and sat for a moment. I wasn't thinking about accomplishments or music or stories; in fact, I wasn't really thinking about anything. And yet there it was: the same alive hum, all on its own, for no reason at all.

Getting up every day and facing the blank page wondering if you have what it takes may gradually drain you of all your confidence, but it has an inherent appeal with which any storyteller is familiar. A hero needs an enemy to fight or a mountain climb, some obstacle to overcome to give his or her journey purpose. Believing you will discover through publication or praise or fabulous sales that you do indeed have what it takes can create the illusion of meaning to your work. Now you're not just telling stories to amuse and inspire yourself and other people, nor to make a living, nor to make the world a slightly brighter place, but ultimately, through hard work and accomplishment, freeing yourself at last from the constant weight of self-doubt.

That drive to prove our value can create a lot of energy. Why, it's almost as if you're writing for your very life. Who would want to live knowing they are lesser-than? As a writer, I know that a story gains momentum the worse the protagonist's dilemma seems to be. If the hero was fine from the start, if they already knew they had everything they needed, there would be no story to tell.

This has been one of the more surprising challenges of learning to see a world where everyone, including me, already has what it takes: It means there's less drama in my life. Where's the real motivation if I have nothing to prove or overcome?

It's a good question. When I was a young man, I was fond of asking, "What's the point?" I was philosophical, and this seemed like a good question to spark some juicy, philosophical writing and conversation. Except it never did. Most of the time I asked it, of course, it wasn't a question at all—it was a lament. I'd feel adrift in my life, no choice better than another, knowing everyone's just going to die, and feeling like everything you'll build will collapse one day anyway. When I felt this way, and I'd ask myself what the point of it all was, I never got answer.

But I also asked it when I was just a little bored, or wanting some interesting problem to solve. What could be more interesting than figuring out the meaning of it all? Again, I could never get further than the question. That it seemed unanswerable was depressing. If it was unanswerable, it meant there was no answer, and there was no point.

Did I ever ask myself what the meaning of it all was while I was writing? No, I did not, at least not when it was going well. I also didn't ask myself what the point of it all was while my brother and I were on stage doing our show, or when I was sitting in my living room in Venice, California, talking to Jen on the phone and knowing I'd have to move to Seattle to be with her. I have never wondered about the meaning of life while I'm caught in its flow, whether writing or talking or just sitting. In this way, life is like a story. I don't really understand a story until I'm telling it. It's why I reread what I wrote the day before, to remind myself what the story feels like and where it's going. So too with life, which makes sense when I'm really in it and not sitting outside of it judging it or complaining about it or wishing it would change and I could be happy.

The difference between my life and a story is I don't actually need drama and problems for it to have meaning. One of the well-kept secrets of writing is that when we're really in The Flow, when we're following that story and not trying to create it all by ourselves, writing isn't hard at all. It's the opposite of hard. And there's also no problem. When I'm in that flow, I'm exactly where I want to be, doing exactly what I want to do, and life is just as I want it to be.

I know this is true, and yet I still have to remind myself that problems and conflicts and challenges have not shaped my life—love has shaped my life. Love was what guided me to write, guided me to Jen, guided me to have children, guided me to my friends, and guided me to write this very book. Love wants nothing other than more love. There is no beginning, middle, or end to it. I'm also never without it. I can ignore it, I can disbelieve it, I can misunderstand it, and yet it will be there for me just the same when I am done moaning and doubting.

So write the story you love.

If you love it, you have what it takes to write it. Period. You may think you need more than that, but you don't. Love will teach you how to write it, will teach you the craft, will teach you how it begins and ends. Let that story be filled with drama and problems and conflicts. You're the author and you love those conflicts and problems. You love them because they teach your hero what he or she needs to learn and because you know they're not real. The reality is the ending, when the problem is solved, when the conflict is over, and now the hero is ready to live life as it was meant to be lived.

> *If you love it, you have what it takes to write it.*

Acknowledgments

I want to thank Nancy Owen Barton for her good humor, optimism, and dedication to what turned out to be a much longer journey than either of us first imagined. You're a good traveling partner.

About the Author

WILLIAM KENOWER is the author of *Fearless Writing: How to Create Boldly and Write with Confidence* and *Write Within Yourself: An Author's Companion*, the editor-in-chief of *Author* magazine, and a sought-after speaker and teacher. His video interviews with hundreds of writers from Nora Ephron to Amy Tan to William Gibson are widely considered the best of their kind on the Internet. He also hosts the podcast *Author-2Author*, where every week he and a different guest discuss the books they write and the lives they lead. To learn more about William, go to williamkenower.com.